# OUR BOYS

# OUR BOYS

## A PERFECT SEASON ON THE PLAINS
## WITH THE SMITH CENTER REDMEN

### JOE DRAPE

TIMES BOOKS

HENRY HOLT AND COMPANY     NEW YORK

Times Books
Henry Holt and Company, LLC
*Publishers since 1866*
175 Fifth Avenue
New York, New York 10010

Henry Holt® is a registered trademark of
Henry Holt and Company, LLC.

Library of Congress Cataloging-in-Publication Data

Drape, Joe.
    Our boys : a perfect season on the plains with the Smith Center Redmen /
Joe Drape.—1st ed.
        p.  cm.
    ISBN: 978-0-8050-8890-8 (alk. paper)
    1. Smith Center High School (Smith Center, Kan.)—Football.   2. Smith Center
(Kan.)—Social life and customs.   I. Title.
    GV959.53.S65D73   2009
    796.332'6209781213—dc22                                          2009026088

Henry Holt books are available for special promotions and
premiums. For details contact: Director, Special Markets.

First Edition 2009

*Designed by Kelly Too*

Printed in the United States of America
3   5   7   9   10   8   6   4   2

*To Mary and Jack,*
*who make me believe*
*that there is no place like home*

# CONTENTS

# THE SMITH CENTER REDMEN

## THE COACHES

ROGER BARTA, head coach

DENNIS HUTCHINSON ("Big Hutch"), chief assistant coach, offensive line and defensive line

MIKE ROGERS, running backs and defensive backs

BROCK HUTCHINSON ("Little Hutch"), defensive coordinator and quarterbacks

TIM WILSON, offensive line and defensive ends

DOUG BOUCHER, strength coach

DARREN SASSE, junior high school coach

DON WICK, offensive line and defensive line

NATE SMITH, quarterbacks and defensive backs

AUSTIN LEWIS, defensive ends

## THE CAPTAINS

KRIS LEHMANN, tight end and outside linebacker

MARSHALL McCALL, running back and free safety

TREVOR REMPE, fullback and defensive lineman

TRENTON TERRILL, offensive lineman and defensive end

## OTHER SENIORS

COLIN DUNTZ, offensive lineman and defensive lineman

ETHAN EASTES, cornerback and quarterback

KALEN MACE, tight end and defensive end

BRIT NIXON, offensive lineman and defensive end

JUSTIN NIXON, offensive lineman and defensive lineman

JOE OSBURN, running back and cornerback

JOEL OSBURN, fullback and outside linebacker

TRAVIS REMPE, quarterback and defensive back

JOHNNY TROY, offensive lineman

CODY TUCKER, offensive lineman and defensive lineman

## JUNIORS

MATT ATWOOD, running back and defensive end

DILLON CORBETT, defensive end and offensive lineman

GARRETT KUHLMANN, tight end, safety, and cornerback

CHASE MCDONALD, tight end, safety, and cornerback

JON OSBURN, running back, safety, and cornerback

TAYLOR RIPPE, tight end, safety, and linebacker

COLT ROGERS, running back and strong safety

JESSE ROUSH, defensive end and offensive lineman

SHAWN STANSBURY, quarterback, safety, and cornerback

LOGAN TUXHORN, middle linebacker and center

SPENCER "YAO MING" VANDERGEISEN, offensive lineman and defensive end

KELLY WIIG, offensive lineman and defensive lineman

## SOPHOMORES

Brock Baxter, quarterback and safety

Curtis Favinger, offensive lineman and defensive lineman

Jake Fisher, offensive lineman and defensive lineman

Zach Herdt, offensive lineman and defensive lineman

Tracy "Chuckie" Hudson, quarterback, safety, and cornerback

Spencer Kirchoff, tight end and defensive end

Aaron McNary, running back and safety

Dereck McNary, running back and outside linebacker

Josh Nixon, offensive lineman and defensive lineman

Willie Overmiller, fullback and middle linebacker

Kaden Roush, offensive lineman and defensive end

Van Tucker, offensive lineman and outside linebacker

## FRESHMEN

Grady Brooks, offensive lineman and defensive lineman

Cole Conaway, offensive lineman and defensive lineman

Nathan Cox, offensive lineman and middle linebacker

Nate Fiester, offensive lineman and defensive lineman

Louis Frasier, offensive lineman, tight end, and defensive end

Alex Hobelmann, quarterback and cornerback

Anden Hughes, tight end and defensive lineman

Truitt Kuhlmann, running back and safety

Brandon Mace, tight end and safety

Cole McDowell, running back and cornerback

Josh McDowell, offensive lineman and defensive end

Trey Molzahn, running back and outside linebacker

CLAY PICKEL, tight end and defensive lineman

MONROE SCHMIDT, tight end and defensive lineman

AARON SELLARS, offensive lineman, outside linebacker, and middle linebacker

BRYCE STANLEY, offensive lineman and defensive lineman

BILLY STOKESBURY, offensive lineman and defensive lineman

KALE TERRILL, center and defensive lineman

JACE WINDER, tight end and defensive end

# OUR BOYS

# INTRODUCTION

*None of this is really about football. . . . What I hope we're doing is sending kids into life who know that every day means something.*
—Roger Barta, November 7, 2007

We were sitting in a locker room that smelled like it had hosted a couple of generations of teenage boys, and Roger Barta was telling me about the high school football program he had built in this town that he loved: Smith Center, Kansas. He was sixty-two years old and wore a red T-shirt that puffed out like a tent over a beach ball–shaped belly. Coach Barta's gray nylon shorts were baggy and hung down to his knees, concealing tree-trunk-sized thighs, his red visor accenting his gray brush cut and silver walrus moustache. His sunglasses hung from a rope and fell atop his stomach. He resembled the actor Wilford Brimley, especially when he spoke in his not-in-a-hurry-honey baritone. He was proof that inspiration comes in all kinds of packages.

Coach Barta was a legend in western Kansas, or so I was told over the course of a three-day visit in November 2007. I was here for the *New York Times* to write about his football team, the Smith Center Redmen. Just a week earlier, his team had scored seventy-two points in the first quarter of a

game, breaking a national record set in 1925. He was amused
that I was in his football complex, having told me the day
before by phone (and with a chuckle) that Smith Center was
harder to get to than one might think.

He was right. I flew into Kansas City, drove north for an
hour to St. Joseph, took a left at Highway 36, and traversed
the old Pony Express route for four hours through northern
Kansas. When I checked into the Buckshot Inn in Smith
Center, I was told I was lucky to get a room, seeing as it was
the opening days of pheasant season and the town's population of 1,931 had swelled with outdoorsmen from the big
cities. When I dropped my bags inside, a sign above my bed
carried the stern instruction: HUNTERS, PLEASE DON'T CLEAN
YOUR BIRDS INSIDE THIS HOTEL ROOM.

By the time I had driven down Main Street and parked in
front of the Second Cup Café, I, too, was amused about being here in the heart of America. In fact, I'd soon discover
that Smith County was the dead center of the continental
United States and had a monument saying so twelve miles
east of here, in Lebanon, Kansas. The county's most famous
contribution to Americana came in 1873, when Dr. Brewster
Higley wrote a poem in a cabin here that evolved into the
song "Home on the Range," which is now a staple of patri-
otic songbooks as well as the state song of Kansas.

*Oh, give me a home where the buffalo roam*
*Where the deer and the antelope play;*
*Where seldom is heard a discouraging word,*
*And the sky is not cloudy all day.*

Outside, above Main Street's wide sidewalks, loudspeakers
piped in easy-listening music. "The Girl from Ipanema" was

playing. Inside the Second Cup Café, every table was filled, as uniformed sheriff's deputies mingled with shirt-sleeved businessmen, and a table full of ladies nodded their hellos to farmers in overalls and gimme caps. No one wore a tie. It was clear that everyone knew everyone here. Once I identified myself and my reason for being in town, the room seemed to relax, and the stories about "our boys" began to unfold. Everyone in the Second Cup, it seemed, had a son or nephew or grandson on the Redmen, but the tales they shared had little to do with their performance on the football field.

They spoke, instead, about the bubblegum cards traded over at the elementary school, with photos of the senior players and cheerleaders, each of whom signed a pledge to remain alcohol-, drug-, and tobacco-free. If they break that promise, they must go to the elementary school to explain to the children why they were kicked off the team and their cards revoked. The café patrons talked about the former players who were now lawyers and doctors in Kansas City and Denver, and how so many of them had worked two or three jobs—just like this current bunch—to save for college.

No one was denying that the Redmen played pretty good football out here on the plains. The current senior class had won fifty-one in a row, three straight championships, and had outscored its opponents 704–0. These seniors had never lost a game in high school, had not let a team *score* on them all year, and were just three games away from capturing their fourth consecutive championship. And, yes, the town was excited; in a couple of days folks would be taping blankets on the metal stands at Hubbard Stadium to secure their seats for the big playoff game against St. Francis.

I have lived and worked as a journalist in Texas, Georgia,

and North Carolina and have done my fair share of "Friday Night Lights" stories. These folks, however, appeared to be the exception rather than the rule for high school football fans. They weren't crazed, and even though it had been a long time since the Redmen had lost, an overwhelming sense of sanity seemed to greet that prospect. No one wanted the team to lose, of course, but I did sense that when the inevitable occurred and the team lost, there would not be any tears or a collective gnashing of the teeth. No, it was enough for folks here that on a whole lot of Friday nights the Redmen were proof that hard work and accountability still meant something.

By all accounts, Coach Barta was the one who set this tone for Smith Center. In his thirty years as head coach, his teams had won 276 football games against only 58 losses, and he had had plenty of offers to move up and on. Instead, he stayed and watched dozens of his boys go on to play college football—including his only son, Brooks, who became a three-year captain at Kansas State and now was coaching high school football in Holton, Kansas. The majority of his former players, however, merely continued their studies and became lawyers and farmers, doctors and newspaper publishers, teachers and coaches. He had coached the fathers of at least a half-dozen members of this team, and a dozen or so children of Redmen alumni were in the pipeline in Smith Center's elementary and junior high schools. For thirty years, his teams had followed the same schedule, were taught the same lingo, and ran the same offense and defense from seventh grade to senior year. Coach Barta valued execution over innovation even if practices became monotonous for his boys.

Joe Windscheffel, the quarterback and the only Redman

ever to start four years, summed it up best. "I can tell you what we're going to do Monday, Tuesday, Wednesday, and Thursday, and what time we're going to do it," he said. "It gets a little boring sometimes, but winning never does."

It was Windscheffel who showed me the town on my first visit and gave me a glimpse into the rituals and mores of the community. He took me to the garage behind his parents' house near the high school, where the Redmen gathered every hour that they were not in school or on the football field. It was their clubhouse, thrown together about how you would expect teenage boys to create a clubhouse: threadbare carpet, a sofa and easy chair cadged from a neighbor, a Ping-Pong table and Carrie Underwood poster front and center, a television equipped with an Xbox and a DVD player, and country music bouncing off the walls even when no one was there. He and I drove past the Jiffy Burger with its gravel lot filled with pickup trucks and stanchion out front proclaiming, THE HOTTEST SPOT IN TOWN. We cruised the Pizza Hut, which also was filled with pickup trucks, and down Main Street to the Looking Glass, a brick-front beauty parlor that sits next to the post office on Court Street. On warm nights, Joe explained, he and his classmates would circle their trucks in front of the Looking Glass, unload couches, and plug a television into an outlet on the side of the building to play video games. Their moms and dads and aunts and uncles would stop by to talk about the game or about bringing in the soybeans, or were just there to check on their kids.

"The nearest McDonald's is ninety miles away," Joe told me. "When you live in a small town, you make your own fun. You also remember that everyone is watching you."

Later that afternoon in his office, Coach Barta was telling me something that I have heard for years from some of the biggest names in college sports, guys who make millions of dollars a year and are featured in television commercials and write motivational books. Coaches talk a good game, especially in the college ranks, where they have to persuade Momma and Daddy to send Junior to their programs. High school coaches, on the other hand, tend to come in three varieties. They are either slick, rah-rah sorts; profane hard guys; or overwhelmed and learning on the job. Coach Barta was none of the above. He was a bear of a man but plainspoken with a touch of Yoda-like wisdom on his tongue.

"What we do around here real well is raise kids," he explained. "In fact, we do such a good job at it—and I'm talking about the parents and community—that they go away to school and succeed, and then pursue opportunities in the bigger cities."

Then he crossed his arms and propped them upon his stomach, and distanced the game of football from what he believed was his true mission in life.

"None of this is really about football," he said. "We're going to get scored on eventually, and lose a game, and that doesn't mean anything. What I hope we're doing is sending kids into life who know that every day means something.

"Sure, we like our football around here," the coach concluded. "But we truly believe it takes a whole town to raise a child, and that's worth a whole lot more."

After I returned to New York and published my story, I found my thoughts frequently returning to Smith Center. I am a native of Kansas City, Missouri, and though I have not lived there in thirty years, I have always counted myself as a midwesterner. My visit to north-central Kansas had validated that view. I had also clicked with the school's principal, Greg Koelsch, and its athletic director, Greg Hobelmann, as well as Coach Barta. I understood their plain speaking and recognized in the young Redmen's "yes, sirs" and "no, sirs" an upbringing much like my own. They struck me as people who woke up each morning intending to make whomever they came across have a better day. Quite simply, I liked them. Coach Barta, too, was someone worth examining more closely. Legends usually are, especially those who seem to stand for the right thing and are far away from the limelight. Coach Barta had already retired from teaching math at the high school, and there was a sense around town that he might quit coaching very soon. He hadn't told anyone his plans, and the consensus was that when the time came, he would end his coaching career with the suddenness of a game-day decision. Coach Barta had built a successful football program, a revered tradition, and, I suspected, a thoughtful worldview out on the plains of Kansas.

He had touched scores of lives. How? And why? I found these questions were worth pursuing.

I also was a new father; my son, Jack, was two years old and was a happy little resident of Manhattan. So was I. Still, it bothered me that he had to trick-or-treat in an apartment building and when we returned to the Midwest for visits, he would see my brother's yard and say, "Look, Daddy, Uncle Tom has a park."

Meanwhile, the Redmen had won their championship, sweeping through the playoffs for their fourth consecutive state title. Their winning streak now stood at fifty-four games. One more perfect season meant that Smith Center would own sixty-seven consecutive victories and five straight titles, both of which would be records for the state of Kansas.

The pressure was going to be enormous, especially on a rising senior class that had not played many meaningful downs in their high school careers. In fact, it did not take long for me to hear about the doubts that surrounded this group of young men, who had not accomplished much on the football field and who failed to inspire confidence in the Smith Center faithful. In 2007, most of them had played late in the second halves of games, when the Redmen usually had a fifty-point lead and their opponents were in a hurry to go home.

My wife, Mary, was a Chicago girl and counted herself a Middle American. We thought, why not try to revisit our midwestern roots? Who doesn't need help raising children? Maybe a season of small-town living might show us a better way. Even if this merely was a midlife crisis, it might be an interesting one.

When I told Coach Barta that I intended to relocate to Smith Center and write a book about the town and the Redmen's 2008 season, he chuckled as he had during our first conversation by phone.

"You know, Joe, we lost twelve seniors and we're really not going to be very good," he said, not altogether convincingly.

When I responded that if they lost, it might be better for the book's narrative, the coach in Coach Barta, the part that didn't like losing, flashed ever so slightly.

"I don't see how that can be," he said.

There was a long pause.

"I do tell our boys it's about the journey," he conceded.

I could hear the smile in his voice.

"We look forward to seeing you back here," he said, "and I promise you'll have the run of the place."

# PART ONE

# HARVEST

# 1

Championships aren't won on the field; they are only played there.

—Team motto for the summer, June 2008

There was nothing but blue sky, miles and miles of it, disturbed only by cotton ball clouds that drifted across a horizon as flat as a tabletop and tiled with the gold, greens, and yellows of healthy crops. A John Deere combine, all shiny metal and sparkling glass, groaned in the distance as it knocked, skinned, and sorted wheat on the first day of what was going to be an abundant and profitable harvest. It had been a perfect summer, and farmers here were looking at an average yield of fifty bushels per acre at a price of anywhere from nine to eleven dollars. Those were big numbers, thanks to another year of healthy rainfall that had kept the farm ponds filled.

Across thousands of acres of western Kansas, the combines would be working into the night as the farmers tuned in to the Kansas City Royals–St. Louis Cardinals game on the radios in the cabs of the big machines. They would work around the clock over the next ten days, trying to bring in their harvest before a hailstorm or another calamity conjured by Mother Nature rendered all their hard work worthless. It was all hands on deck as eight-year-old grandsons and grown sons with desk jobs in Omaha or Topeka or Wichita came home and took turns driving the grain cart and bringing the crop in.

Jay Overmiller, forty-seven years old, was inside his New Holland Combine, a $350,000 piece of machinery as vital to a farmer as an atom splitter is to a nuclear physicist. In many ways it was comparable: the computer screen told him the moisture of the grain—anything below 13 percent was good—and how many bushels of wheat he was getting per acre (fifty to seventy), as well as his fuel efficiency. Jay could even put the combine on automatic pilot if he wanted, and close his eyes and listen to satellite radio. He also had about a half-million dollars' worth of sprayers and tractors that he kept in immaculate condition. He had put a lot of money into these machines, but he still wasn't sure whether he believed that farmers were about to become the new millionaires, as many financial types predicted.

"I don't know what my net worth is day-to-day," he said. "I'm at the mercy of the guys who don't have the wheat in their hands determining how much what I've got in my bins is worth."

He had been up at dawn for the twenty-minute drive to his parents' house, where his mother, Jean, had breakfast ready for him, just as when Jay was a boy. His oldest son, Willie, was meeting him there after he finished lifting weights at Smith Center High School. Willie would be a sophomore when school began—and a fullback on the Redmen even sooner, when preseason camp started in mid-August.

"I'm one of those lucky guys who have coffee every morning with Mom and Dad," Jay said.

For the next fifteen hours, and over the next ten or so days of the wheat harvest, the Overmillers would choreograph an intricate ballet performed by giant farm machinery and aided by chutes and ladders as they farmed their three thousand acres. Jay bumped along in the combine until its lights started flashing, signaling to Willie that it was almost full of wheat. Willie then pulled alongside with the grain cart as Jay swung the chute overhead and let the wheat fall into the cart—neither one of them slowing down a bit. Willie took the load to Bill Overmiller—Jay's dad, his grandfather—who waited on a gravel farm road with a truck. Another chute completed the transfer. Bill took the wheat to a bin, where a conveyor ladder sucked and dumped it once more.

As soon as the wheat harvest was over, the countdown to Smith Center's football season began in earnest. Jay had played for Coach Barta's very first team in 1978 and had been one of the town's early stars. He loved the game and was eager to watch Willie, as well as his younger boys, Trevor and Gavin, grow up under the coach's tutelage.

When Willie was in fourth grade, he asked Jay to build a regulation goalpost in the field in front of their home. Jay borrowed Coach Barta's rulebook and constructed a goalpost to specifications. It rose in front of the family's white barn with fifty yards of soft, manicured grass rolled out before it. The field had hosted pickup games ever since for Smith Center's boys, from ages four to fifteen. The goalpost looked as if it belonged here among the wheat and milo and soybeans every bit as much as the silver grain bins and turning windmills. Jay had taught Willie as much as he could; now it was the coach's turn. He hoped Coach Barta would still be around when Trevor, thirteen, got to the high school, and yes, even eleven-year-old Gavin.

At least he got Willie to him.

I was eager for football season, too, and was in town to find a place to live as well as to reintroduce myself to as many Redmen as I could find. Like most small towns on the plains, Smith Center had struggled to retain its population. In 1900, more than 16,300 people inhabited Smith County, a number that had slowly dwindled as advanced farming techniques made human labor less necessary. As much of a marvel as it was to watch three generations of Overmillers bring in the wheat, precision farming also had run off too many folks who did not have the financial wherewithal to make the transition.

It was the "dirty thirties," as the old folks here still call it, however, that had sent people fleeing from Smith County in torrents. It was beyond dry, and dusty when tons upon tons of topsoil were blown off barren fields and carried in storm clouds for hundreds of miles. Southeastern Colorado, southwest Kansas, and the panhandles of Oklahoma and Texas became the epicenter of dust storms. In 1932, fourteen of them were recorded on the plains. In 1933, there were thirty-eight. By 1934, it was estimated that 100 million acres of farmland had lost all or most of the topsoil to the winds. In the early spring of 1935, there had been weeks of dust storms, but the cloud that appeared on the horizon on Sunday, April 14, 1935, was the worst. Winds were clocked at sixty miles per hour, and "Black Sunday" introduced a new term to our national lexicon: *the Dust Bowl.*

On the same day that dust was swirling along America's Great Plains, Hugh Hammond Bennett, an adviser to President Franklin Delano Roosevelt, was preparing to testify before Congress about the need for soil conservation legislation. Mother Nature seconded his argument when a dust storm rolled from the heart of America into the nation's capital. "This, gentlemen, is what I have been talking about," Bennett would tell Congress.

It was a theatrical flourish, and Congress, indeed, passed the Soil Conservation Act. But it was too late to reverse the damage inflicted on places like Smith County. By 1940, the county had lost more than a third of its population, as only 10,582 remained. It has been hemorrhaging population ever since; today about 4,500 people live in the county, and over the years clothing and sporting goods stores, dry cleaners, and all major manufacturing have disappeared. Smith County's annual per capita income is only $14,983, which makes it the fifth poorest of the state's 105 counties.

Good economic news is still hard to come by. More than fifty people had recently been laid off at Peterson Industries, which manufactures trailers and campers and is Smith County's second-largest employer behind the school district. Thirty-six miles west of here in Phillipsburg, the Brooke Corporation, an insurance and financial services company founded by a Smith Center banker, was on the verge of bankruptcy and about to put two hundred people out of work, many of them from Smith County.

Even the Transcendental Meditation movement appeared to be giving up on its plan to bring anywhere from ten thousand to forty thousand students to the Maharishi Central University that had been under construction on three hundred acres ten miles north of town. No one was particularly thrilled when the group announced in 2006 its plan to build a series of peace palaces and an organic farm. Over the past two years, however, the group's leaders had been a presence in town, and construction crews worked on more than a half-dozen buildings.

No more. It had been months since anyone had seen the "TMers," as they were known, and the metal frames of their buildings dotted the countryside like the carcasses of picked-over scarecrows. In fact, no one had left much behind in Smith County. There were hollowed-out farmhouses overgrown with Indian grass that were home to pheasants and quail and the occasional methamphetamine laboratory.

This was my third visit since the previous November, and I had yet to secure a place to live. It was an inventory problem; rentals were nonexistent, and I counted just nine homes for sale. I had been able to look at only one dwelling, a duplex that even by Manhattan standards was far too small. Bob Rethorst, one of the two real estate agents in town, counseled patience and assured me that something would turn up. He was eighty-two years old, a six-foot, four-inch hulk of a man with snow-white hair who inspired confidence. So I did as I was told and didn't worry.

While the Kansas plains at dusk during harvest offer about as majestic a tableau as you can conjure, the town of Smith Center does not turn any heads at first blush. Highway 36, which spans the county east–west, is the town's northern border. The speed limit drops from sixty-five to forty-five miles per hour at the first sight of the John Deere tractors that stand sentry and ready for sale at Jones Machinery to the east of town, and at Landmark Implements to its west.

In between them are the Buckshot Inn and two other motels, the Prairie Winds and U.S. Center. There is a boarded-up bowling alley and a jumble of tin and wood buildings with ramshackle signs advertising body and auto repair shops. The Jiffy Burger is south of Highway 36 and fronts Smith Center High School, and the Pizza Hut and

Paul's Café and Dining Room are on the highway's north side.

There is a blinking yellow light at the intersection of Highway 281, which runs north–south from Nebraska to Oklahoma, and which for ten blocks is Smith Center's Main Street. Clapboard ranch houses with stone basements lead into the business district and past brick buildings to the railroad tracks and the grain elevator. Here, the Smith Center Co-op Elevator sprouts drums and an eight-pack of white turrets from a gravel parking lot and is the first thing anyone sees from far away on the highway. It looks like a medieval castle.

As you get closer, however, another image takes precedence: rising from wheat fields and surrounded by farm machinery are the lights of a football stadium, the Hubbard football complex. It has helped Smith County endure decades of people and businesses leaving, as well as years of drought that tested the hardiest of farmers. It is the home of the Redmen, who for a long time now have delivered what TM's Eastern thinkers had promised but apparently abandoned: peace and harmony.

The Redmen's football complex sits on a street called Roger Barta Way. In the wake of the Redmen's winning streak and the national attention it commanded, the Smith Center City Council decided to name the road to the high school after its football coach and retired math teacher. Coach Barta usually caught wind of such machinations, but he was genuinely surprised when the decision was announced at a high school basketball game the previous winter. He was honored, but not altogether comfortable with it. He was conscious of the fact that athletics most often trumped academics in communities, large and small, and he did not want to add to that perception. He hoped that a street near the school might be named for his friend and colleague Demetre Evangelidis when the latter retired. "Mr. E," as the students called him, had taught chemistry for twenty-five years at Smith Center High School and was considered one of the most committed and effective teachers in the region.

Even in the summer, Smith Center knew where its young people were—at the high school. They were there this evening on the last day of June, a hundred of them, boys and girls from the seventh to twelfth grades, lifting barbells in the weight room and running sprints out on the back lawn. Kids swarmed the parking lot on the south and east sides of the high school, looking for some relief from the suffocating ninety-two-degree heat.

Among them was Marshall McCall. He was hoarse and sniffled and tried to clean up after a nose that was leaking at a far greater rate than his sweat. He was a smart, well-mannered seventeen-year-old and wiped his nose with his T-shirt discreetly when he hoped no one was looking. Marshall was supposed to be at wrestling camp at the University of Nebraska, but he had been battling a virus savage enough to strip ten pounds off his five-foot, ten-inch frame over the past three days. Marshall had prolonged his illness by working through the virus, showing up each morning for his summer job as a plumbers' assistant and trench-and-grave digger. Now he was pale, raccoon-eyed, and looked nothing like the square-shouldered All-American Opie that he was a few days ago.

Marshall should have been home in bed. Instead, he headed for the practice field just outside the weight room for agility drills with a dozen of his football teammates in tow. Marshall was a senior and one of four captains elected by his peers at the beginning of the summer to lead the Red-men to what was destined to be a record-breaking year. No, it had the potential to be an immortal year.

Marshall was hoping to get a scholarship to play foot-ball in college, but it was not something he could count on. Healthy and in shape, he was barely 165 pounds, and on his best day he ran the forty-yard dash in 4.7 seconds, which is neither big nor fast enough to entice big-time Division I football coaches to Smith Center. He knew it, and so did his parents. They had decided that Marshall should apply early to the state schools—the University of Kansas, Kansas State, and Fort Hays State—so he could concentrate on his senior year, and perhaps his last season of football, and they could be assured their son had somewhere to go to college.

Marshall worked from 7:30 a.m. to 6:00 p.m., saved his money, and prayed at night that he might get a partial scholar-ship to a smaller school like Sterling College, which was two hours due south, or perhaps Washburn University in Topeka, where his dad had played football.

Marshall knew that saving for college meant digging the hole where the father of his junior high school football coach, Darren Sasse, was going to be laid to rest, putting on a coat and tie for the funeral, and then shedding both to shovel dirt on the casket after the service. He had done just that re-cently, and it was OK with him. It beat the hell out of getting itchy baling hay, as he had done six previous summers, in the scorching heat that turned the plains of Kansas into a microwave where the only relief was an overheated breeze that felt like it packed darts.

Marshall's boss, Tracy Kingsbury, had told him that grave digging was upholding a sacred trust in a town that was held together by a love for these flatlands, an abiding respect for its heritage, and empathy for the struggles its families had shared over generations.

Really, Kingsbury told him, it was "the ultimate job security."

The ubiquitous death notices in the *Smith County Pioneer* proved Kingsbury right. For the last fifteen years there has been a run on death here. The Hill, as the cemetery north of town is known, was becoming one of Smith County's few overcrowded neighborhoods, increasing its occupancy at the rate of 125 new residents a year, and prompting the old folks of Smith Center to hold their young people close as long as possible.

At the high school this evening, the weight room was full, and iron dumbbells clanged to the beat of loud heavy-metal music. Next door in the gym, applause echoed and a referee's whistle pierced the air, giving rhythm to a summer volleyball tournament.

Outside on the practice field, Marshall lined up orange cones while Doug Boucher, a strength coach, dragged out a rectangular rack divided in squares for the boys to high-step through. Suddenly, a squeal of tires and the crunch of flying gravel interrupted the quiet. A yellow Sierra Spider spotted with rust fishtailed near the practice field.

"Slow down, son," bellowed Boucher.

Marshall and his teammates snapped their heads to the parking lot, where Dillon Corbett—all six feet, two inches of him—unfolded himself from the little car. He smiled a goofy grin and took a seat on the grass to lace up his football cleats.

Boucher shook his head, bewildered.

"Son, do you want kill somebody?" he asked. He did not wait for an answer. "Have some sense, boy."

*Boom!* A firecracker exploded in the gravel, startling Dillon and Marshall and the rest of the Redmen. Kirk Palmer grinned maniacally from inside his pickup truck. Last year, he was the Redmen's All-State center and middle linebacker. In a couple of weeks, he was off to Butler Junior College to continue his football career. He had been haunting the weight room all summer, putting another twenty pounds of granite on his five-foot, ten-inch frame. Boucher stared at him.

"Kids," he said, like it was the word for the plague.

Marshall hustled his fellow Redmen in line and started them zigzagging around the cones. He didn't want to endure another tongue-lashing. Boucher had braced Marshall two weeks ago about his leadership qualities, about his fellow captains' ability to lead, about the stones this senior class might, or might not, possess.

"Get out of here," Boucher told Palmer. The former Redmen star gunned his pickup and blew out of the parking lot.

Doug Boucher watched the dust settle with a slight smile. At forty-five years old, he still cut an intimidating figure despite the crow's feet around his eyes and the gray on his temples and streaked in his mustache. He had a barrel chest and arms that looked pulled through with steel cable. Besides being a certified strength coach, he was a graduate of Kansas State and a substitute teacher. Until recently, however, he had been a hog farmer, a profession that he enjoyed all right but one that took its toll. Both his knees were now shot, and after twenty years and hundreds of sows banging into them, he walked stiffly from side to side and sometimes required prescription painkillers.

He had played quarterback for the Redmen, taking them

to the state finals in 1979, which was Coach Barta's second season as head coach. His son, David, won a championship in 2004 as a linebacker on the team that started the current winning streak.

Boucher passed on what he had worked hard late in his life to learn about strength conditioning; the kids, in turn, were helping him to get better as a teacher. He was worried about this senior class, however, and when Marshall was the only one who showed up to lift a few weeks ago, Boucher told him how concerned he was.

He pointed to the poster board, where all fifty-plus names of the Smith Center football team were listed and followed by grids charting their attendance. Instead of colored-in squares showing perfect attendance, Boucher pointed at the white spots, way too many of them. He also nodded to the blackboard where the motto for the summer had been scrawled: CHAMPIONSHIPS AREN'T WON ON THE FIELD; THEY ARE ONLY PLAYED THERE, it read. THEY ARE DECIDED BEFORE THAT RIGHT HERE.

"Look at them," Boucher said to Marshall, glancing toward the weight room.

Joe Windscheffel, Drew Joy, Grady Godsey, Matt Seemann, Kerby Rice, and Kirk Palmer—nearly every player from last year's senior class—were sweating beneath barbells, encouraging one another. Since junior high school, that group of graduating seniors had never lost a football game. They worked like beasts, loved each other like brothers, and nine of them had received scholarships to play football—one, Braden Wilson, at Kansas State in Division I.

Boucher almost wanted to throw them out of the weight room. Their accomplishments had been too big and had overshadowed Marshall and his classmates.

"Those are the guys that have won fifty-four games in a row and four championships," Boucher told Marshall. "Those are their numbers. Those memories belong to them."

Then Boucher pulled Marshall into the coach's office and told him to sit down. He sat on the desk and laid out his, the coaching staff's, and much of the town's doubts about the 2008 Redmen.

"What matters now, Marshall, are the next thirteen games and the next Kansas state championship," Boucher told him. "Where are your fellow captains, where are the seniors? No one here is worried about the talent you guys have, and I know, for the most part, you guys give great effort. But I'm worried about the seniors' ability to lead this team. You have been standing in the shadows of those guys outside so long, I'm not sure you know how to do anything yourself.

"You guys need to step into the sunshine and lead this team. You need to lead by your work ethic and your example. You need to become more verbal. Marshall, you need to figure this stuff out real soon, or it is going to be a very long season."

Marshall shifted in his seat, and Boucher softened.

"Look, my son, David, talks about his 2004 championship team like it was the greatest team in the history of Smith Center football," he said. "There are seniors from seven previous championship teams around here that can have that argument. It's a small fraternity. I'm not even in it. I want you guys to be the eighth."

Marshall was the right senior for Boucher to light a fire under. He was an oldest child and possessed those qualities number-one sons often possess: earnestness and determination mixed with doubt and an eagerness to please. Marshall was a worrier. He knew that he and his fellow seniors were carrying a heavy load and that it was already getting to them. Trevor Rempe, another senior captain and one of the team's most fearless players, had been quoted in a preseason magazine story that the Redmen would probably be underdogs in many of their games, and he indicated that he and his teammates were ready to accept a defeat, preferably in the regular season rather than in the playoffs.

"We won't hang our heads, but it will hurt," Trevor had told John Baetz, the editor of the magazine *Kansas Pregame*, the bible of Kansas high school football junkies. The admission was all the more surprising because Baetz was a Smith Center native and a former Redman himself. "But we can still win a fifth state championship even though we wouldn't be undefeated," Trevor said.

In Smith Center, Trevor's remarks were chalked up as further evidence of the senior class's lack of seasoning. Everywhere else in Kansas, it was evidence that these Redmen lacked heart.

Like the New York Yankees or the Fighting Irish of Notre Dame, Smith Center football was a love-them-or-loathe-them proposition in the state of Kansas. Their tradition of success had inspired envy, and the recent onslaught of national media had forged a deep-seated envy that often became ugly on Internet message boards. The attention hadn't subsided, either. The previous month, *Sports Illustrated* had written about Smith Center and ran a quarter-page photograph of the school's athletes atop a combine.

Marshall understood that last year's seniors had eclipsed his class. The *Smith County Pioneer*, the local weekly newspaper, referred to the four-time champions as the "best class in Smith Center's storied past, and arguably the best ever in Kansas high school football." In the weight room next to

Marshall and his teammates, Windscheffel, Wilson, Palmer, and the rest looked like NFL players. They racked weight after weight noisily on the free bars and sneered at the puny amount of poundage Marshall and his classmates slid on their bars.

It was just the latest indignity. Not only had Marshall's class not been very good in junior high school, but they also drew attention to themselves for all the wrong reasons. In eighth grade, they showed up for the first game of the season wearing eye black and wristbands up to their elbows, and promptly got blown out. Coach Sasse made them lose the accessories, but their insecurities didn't disappear and they finished a middling 3–4. Now, they were known mainly for following the orders and riding the coattails of the class ahead of them.

For the three previous years, the team's clubhouse was in Joe Windscheffel's garage. Joe and the others ruled the Ping-Pong table. They chose the movies the team watched on the eve of each game.

They led; everyone else followed.

Marshall did not want to be on the team that ended the Redmen's winning streak. As he left Boucher, he ran into one of his best friends and teammate, Colt Rogers, in the parking lot, and told him that word was getting out that the streak was in danger even though they hadn't even put on their pads yet.

Colt, also seventeen years old, was barely five foot three and 135 pounds, but he was perhaps the most fearsome competitor in western Kansas. In addition to having played on two state football title teams, Colt was 70–0 as a wrestler and a two-time state champion. He also was a member of Smith Center's 400-meter relay team that held the state title in track. Colt was only a junior and had not been elected a captain. He was, however, a natural leader.

He and Marshall set out to find their fellow Redmen and to get each of them to commit to lifting together in the evenings. They started at the Jiffy Burger, where they found a half-dozen of their teammates. They got the message to Spencer VanderGeisen, the tallest boy in town at six foot five (everybody called him "Yao Ming"), and to "Chuckie," who was really named Tracy Hudson, but whose red hair, freckles, and appetite for mischief reminded his teammates of the Chuckie doll from the horror movie series. The word went out as well to Trevor Rempe and his twin brother, Travis; to the Osburn brothers, Joe, Jon, and Joel; to the Tuckers, Cody and Van; to the McNary twins, Aaron and Dereck; and to Jesse and Kaden Roush.

Marshall and Colt cruised along Main Street and spotted Dillon Corbett's yellow Spider in front of the movie house. They found him front and center with a bucket of popcorn, hauled him from his seat, out of the theater, and onto the sidewalk. They told him what they were telling everyone: from now on, it's going to be 100 percent attendance at the evening session.

On this sweltering evening in June, Marshall was pleased by the sight of the Redmen high-stepping through the grid, sweat loosening the hard muscles they had spent the previous hour strengthening on bench presses and squat machines. But he also knew that just as many of his teammates were not here, including two seniors the Redmen desperately needed in the fall. Where were Justin Nixon and Joe Osburn? Justin, a 350-pound lineman, was a two-year starter who had not been here all summer, and Joe, the Redmen's fastest running back, had barely shown up.

Even as a seventh grader, Marshall had wanted to be a leader, the kind of guy others looked to for encouragement and direction. He was winded, weak, and not over his virus, but he was here. Being with his teammates, he knew, was the best medicine for him.

# 2

Together we are champions.

—Roger Barta, August 18, 2008

"It's a great day to be a Redman, isn't it guys," said Coach Barta.

It was a statement rather than a question. It was 6:30 a.m., and before him were fifty-six bleary-eyed high school students ready for the first practice of the season, and of the day. They would be coming back at 6:00 p.m.

The freshmen sat on the cement floor of the Hubbard football complex, while the upperclassmen had stools propped in front of their lockers. Each of them wore gym shorts and white practice jerseys and held their red Smith Center helmets in their laps. The freshmen had concave chests or jiggled with baby fat. Some were battling acne for the first time. About a half-dozen of them tried to telegraph their fierce intentions (or hide their fearful thoughts) by cutting their hair into Mohawks. Unfortunately, they were shaped like tails that made them look more like skunks than warriors.

The sophomores, too, were still going through puberty

and had narrow shoulders and coat-rack frames. They were not as wide-eyed as the freshmen, but the perplexed looks on their faces and the furtive glances that passed between them betrayed the fact that they did not quite consider themselves football players.

Only the juniors and seniors appeared comfortable, even happy, to be up in the morning dark for the first day of football practice. They had gotten here early and cranked up the stereo so that metal music reverberated throughout this cinderblock building. Their wrists and ankles were taped, and they wore sleeveless form-fitting undershirts to show off the ripped biceps and abdominal muscles they had sculpted over their years in the Redmen weight-lifting program. They looked eager to hit the practice field. They embraced the ritual that was under way on high school practice fields all over the nation: preseason training camp, two weeks of twice-a-day practices.

Training camp is meant to forge camaraderie through communal misery. There is a reason coaches and broadcasters fall back on metaphors about war when they talk about football—no matter how inappropriate they sound in this day and age. Football is a game of tactics, where dominance is measured by ground gained or lost, where the individual must work in concert with others to be successful. It is the only American sport where violence, sacrifice, and pain are celebrated and must be dished out and endured to be victorious. Like military boot camp, training camp is about breaking down the minds and bodies of the individuals in order to begin putting them back together as a group. So each morning and each afternoon on these arid plains, the Redmen would run off their summer fun beneath a blazing sun until they were breathing hard and sweating off pounds.

Coach Barta paced in front of the blackboard. There were some *X*'s and *O*'s on it, but mostly it was filled with commonsense admonishments.

Everyone must shower to avoid Staph infection.
Drink Water: You want clear urine. If yellow, drink more.

This locker room was Coach Barta's classroom, and the practice field was his laboratory, as it had been for longer than he wanted to remember. He was both God and Buddha here—at once almighty and, he hoped, the guide to a lifetime of serenity and higher purpose. He had a few notes jotted down on a piece of paper. It did not matter that he had lived through thirty previous opening days of training camp. He still had butterflies. Every one of his teams was different, and, as he preached to his players, Coach Barta enjoyed the journey that began here each August. And for the past four years that journey had been completed at the end of November with his kids hoisting the Kansas state 2A championship trophy aloft.

The tone for the next four months would be laid out here today over two practice sessions. The lessons of love, respect, and becoming a better man each day, he hoped, would last a lifetime. It would be hammered home day after day until the football season was ended or another championship earned.

"OK, everyone grab their helmets, and let's read it together," Coach Barta commanded.

The Redmen turned their helmets backward in their laps and read in unison the warning label required to be there by the National Operating Committee on Standards for Athletic Equipment.

No helmet can prevent all head or any neck injuries a player might receive while participating in football. Do not use this helmet to butt, ram, or spear an opposing player. This is in violation of the football rules and such use can result in severe head or neck injuries, paralysis, or death to you and possible injury to your opponent.

Coach Barta let the ominous words sink in with his players.

"Now you guys know that being out here, you are taking on an assumption of risk," he said. "This is a rough game, you know that. It is a game where violence is allowed. But if you guys listen to the coaches in here and really try to use proper technique, you're going to be OK. In fact, it's thirty-one times safer to play football than it is to drive a car. You know that, right?"

He let that fact linger out there in the silence. No one doubted its veracity because Barta had been a math teacher. He was a coach first, however, and over the course of the season he would utter similar absolutes without really knowing—or caring—if they were 100 percent true.

"Now we'll talk later tonight about some other important things," he continued, "but let's get out there now and have a fast and efficient practice. We want to have fun, too. So let's go."

The rhythm of fifty-six pairs of cleats picked up tempo and was punctuated by whoops and war cries as the Redmen filed out of the locker room and into the darkness for the 2008 team's first football practice. It was going to be virtually the same practice experienced by thirty previous Smith Center teams. The typed practice schedule, folded lengthwise in half and stuck in the back pockets of Coach

Barta and each member of his staff, made certain of it. It set out a minute-by-minute schedule of drills, breakout groups, and water breaks the team would perform over the next two hours.

There was no mistaking this group of Redmen for a college team. They were boys, scared ones. Many were so wide-eyed beneath their helmets that you wanted to look behind you and see if there was a semitruck bearing down on them. When Bobby Knight set the record for the most victories in NCAA Division I college basketball, he told me that he would have been far more impressed with himself if he had been the winningest coach in high school basketball.

"'That's where the real coaching is done," he said. "You take the talent that lives in the area and mold them into a team."

Coach Barta's .825 winning percentage at Smith Center was evidence that he knew how to build a team and a program out of the boys who called this outpost of north-central Kansas home. He professed that it was built on the hard work of tough kids and honed by rote and repetition. It began right here at the Redmen's first practice with fifteen minutes of stretching. The stretching focused the boys, as did the sprints that followed.

Soon, sweat was pouring down their smiling faces, and the chatter picked up.

"Everywhere we go-oo," Trevor Rempe called out in sing-song melody.

"*Everywhere we go-oo,*" his teammates echoed with a full throat.

"People want to kno-ow."

"*People want to kno-ow.*"

"Whooo we are."

"*Whooo we are.*"

"So we tell them."

"*So we tell them.*"

Both the calls and responses were picking up steam.

"We are the Red-Men."

"*We are the Red-Men.*"

"The mighty, mighty Red-Men."

"*The mighty, mighty Red-Men.*"

When Trevor growled the final chorus, the players' voices reached a crescendo.

"OOOH, AAAH, how does it feel?"

"*OOOH, AAAH, it feels good.*"

"OOOH, AAAH, how does it feel?"

"*OOOH, AAAH, it feels good.*"

"OOOH, AAAH, how does it feel?"

"*OOOH, AAAH, it feels good.*"

Joyful whoops and clapping followed, and even the frightened freshmen were smiling ear-to-ear. Now it was real that football season was under way, and it was clear the boys had surrendered to a game and a ritual that they truly loved.

The first practice rolled downhill from there. Even though no one was in pads, the Redmen queued up in parallel lines and ran at an angle toward each other for form tackling drills. The defender was supposed to aim his head across the ball carrier's body, lock his arms around the runner's lower body, and drive through with his hips. They did, one after another, lifting each other three feet off the ground and carrying them another five before dropping them back on their feet. As the Redmen gained energy, the coaching staff harnessed it and gave it purpose.

"Eyes up, thumbs up, drive through the ball," shouted Coach Brock Hutchinson, the defensive coordinator, who had played here and graduated in 1993. "That's it. That's it."

When the sun finally peeked over the plains in the east, bathing the field in a rouge halo, the team broke up by positions. Coach Mike Rogers, who had graduated from Smith Center High School in 1984 and played at the University of Kansas, herded the running backs into the east corner of the practice field, which abutted a wheat field. He handed out blocking dummies and had each player run through a gauntlet of teammates who tried to knock the ball out of his hands.

"You're holding it too loose," he barked. "You keep it tight. If you drop the ball, you're giving me twenty push-ups."

Dennis Hutchinson and Tim Wilson put the linemen through crouch, read, and react drills on the west end of the field. Coach Hutchinson, or Big Hutch, was Brock's father and had been with Coach Barta for each of his thirty years here. Coach Wilson had been an offensive lineman for the Redmen until graduating in 1990, and he was starting his eighth season as a coach here, which made him the newest member of the staff.

In the middle of the field, Coach Barta crouched like a linebacker, his hands resting on his thighs, watching a quartet of fullbacks take handoffs from a line of quarterbacks.

"I coach the fullbacks because they are the most important position on the team," Barta told them. "When you guys do what you're supposed to, our offense meshes."

The coach was not lying to his fullbacks. The Redmen ran an extraordinarily simple offense that had morphed into what was now called the Barta-Bone. It was an offshoot of the Wishbone, which was invented in 1968 by Emory Bellard, the offensive coordinator at the University of Texas.

The Longhorns and their rival, the Oklahoma Sooners, popularized the offense, which featured three running backs, in the 1970s and 1980s. Over the years, there have been volumes written about its practice and theory. In laymen's terms, the Wishbone has the quarterback taking the snap under center, with a fullback close behind him, and two halfbacks farther back and flanked to either side, thus the alignment of the four backs make an inverted Y, or wishbone shape. It sets up the triple option, a running play where the fullback, quarterback, or one of the halfbacks ends up carrying the ball.

Coach Barta had simplified it even further: the Redmen ran the fullback up the middle and the halfbacks off the tackles. They rarely pitched out for a sweep or passed the ball. They never kicked an extra point, preferring to try for two points by running the ball into the end zone from the 3-yard line. Smith Center routinely averaged nine yards per carry for a season—you do the math. Field goals? They were attempted rarely and only when the Redmen were so far ahead that Coach Barta was trying not to run up the score.

The Redmen were a power football team, pure and simple. Coach Barta believed that if the Redmen ran the offense crisply, the opposing defense would have no idea who had the ball and would be forced to tackle four players on each play. It was not only frustrating for defenses but also exhausting.

"I don't care about speed; I care about execution," Coach Barta told his fullbacks. "I want the whole defense sucking in on the fullback. You run hard through the hole whether you got the ball or not. Dip your shoulder and hit someone. You got to sell them."

Rarely did the scripted practice sheet come out of the coaches' back pockets. They had been together a long time and moved in concert like hands on a clock, silently and precisely. Mike Rogers had the backs at the water break first. They were on one knee, huffing and puffing, as the girls' volleyball team, at least fifty of them, ran past the practice field on their way to the track.

"Get up there, McCall," Marshall shouted to his younger sister, Hallie. "You're better than that."

Colt Rogers and Travis and Trevor Rempe laughed as Hallie McCall ran by, trailing her teammates. She was a freshman, and her big brother, true to his nature, was worried about her. She was a sharp student and a decent athlete. More worrisome was that Hallie was pretty and sociable. Marshall knew what high school boys wanted, and reminded his teammates again that they were to stay away from his little sister. When they laughed at him, he shrugged.

"It's going to be a tough year," he said.

It also was going to be a monastic autumn for Marshall and some of the Redmen. For years now, Smith Center players had taken their football season seriously. The pledge each player made not to drink or smoke or do drugs was real. Neither Coach Barta nor anyone else at the high school was naive enough to believe that alcohol had not found its way into the student body. It's perhaps more rare than it is in bigger cities because of the lack of opportunities. The town has only one bar and one liquor store. It's impossible to walk into a convenience store to buy beer even with the best fake identification and expect not to know anyone inside, especially if you are a high school student. Still, drinking happens, out in the woods and desolate farmland. Perhaps the best evidence of the pledge's effectiveness is that following the last couple of football seasons no player had been involved in an alcohol incident.

This year's senior class, however, had taken their communal dedication to a successful football season a step further. They were not exactly banning girls from their lives, but they intended to greatly limit the time they spent with them. This vow of austerity was agreed upon—of all places—in the showers. No one can remember for sure how it began, but after a summer workout as the guys discussed the challenges ahead of them and the goals they wanted to achieve, it became clear that they needed to make a commitment.

"We were talking about how football just sort of takes over everything else," Marshall said.

By the time training camp started, Trevor Rempe had broken up with his girlfriend outright, and several other starters were still recovering from the difficult conversations they tried to have with theirs. Marshall had it easier than most because his girlfriend, Brittni Robison, was a freshman at Cloud Community College in Concordia, Kansas, which was more than an hour away. Brittni also was a volleyball player with her own busy competitive schedule. Still, even she thought it was odd when Marshall suggested they see each other only once a week, on Sunday.

As practice began to wind down, the coaching staff was in a good mood. They, too, were happy to be on familiar ground, teaching another group of kids a game they cared about deeply.

Big Hutch was lecturing the linemen about technique, making them antsy and inadvertently keeping them away from the water. His son, Brock, or Little Hutch, could not resist twisting the needle into his father.

"It's the first day of practice," he said. "You trying to do all your coaching for the year?"

"I'm just trying to stay ahead of you young geniuses," Big Hutch replied.

At 8:30 a.m., Coach Barta walked to the middle of the field and raised his hand, and the Redmen sprinted to him from the four corners of the practice field. They clapped rhythmically until Coach Barta put one finger in the air.

"Whooo," they said in unison, a muted war cry, and then snapped to attention.

The Redmen were out of breath as they gathered around the coach. He listened to them huff and puff.

"That's the sound of hard work," he said. "That was a good first practice. I really believe that you can be a smart team, a fast team. We're going to have to work at it, and our goal each day is to get just a little bit better. It's our goal as a football team, and it should be yours as a student and a son and a brother and a citizen. Every day if you try to become a little bit better, you're going to become a better man."

He paused and looked around the circle.

"We'll see you back here tonight," he said. "Good job."

————

The coaches' office in the Hubbard complex was not much to look at—blue lockers on one wall and across from them a long desk fashioned from plywood and file cabinets. Its top was buried under papers and littered with liters of soda. Beneath it were boxes full of jerseys and T-shirts and rolls of tape. Scouting reports dating back five years were in red binders and lined the shelves.

Coach Barta knew they were lucky to have this space. These offices and the stadium were built with the money of R. D. Hubbard, who had grown up directly across the street from here and was Smith Center High School's biggest benefactor. R.D. had graduated from Smith Center High in 1953 and was briefly a high school basketball coach before deciding that there must be a better way than living in a twenty-seven-foot-trailer and making $3,600 a year. In the years since, he had built a glass company, bought casinos and racetracks, and created a foundation that gave away millions annually to help students in Kansas and New Mexico, where he now lived.

Coach Barta and his staff gathered here a half hour before practice each day and pulled their desk chairs into a circle to needle each other and muse a little about the state of the team. The discussion rarely rose to the level of grand strategy sessions.

Coach Barta and Big Hutch were both retired from teaching, and if they looked like they had just rolled out of bed from naps it was because they had. In fact, once training camp was over, much of Coach Barta's day was built around naps. He arose each morning to have breakfast with his wife, Pam, who was the director of Smith Center's Community Development. He went back to bed as soon as she left for work, but not before setting the alarm so he could walk Tootsie, the family shih tzu, and look alert when Pam returned for lunch. "Nothing good happens before noon," he would growl to his staff when they teased him.

Coach Barta would get one more nap in before heading to the high school about two o'clock in the afternoon. There he hunkered down in what the ladies in the school office called the "man-cave," and what the coaching staff called the "NASA lab." It actually was a well-turned-out computer and media lab, where video could be cut for scouting reports and software programs organized and turned into strategy. R. D. Hubbard had paid for that as well.

Big Hutch barely set foot in the high school anymore. He had been a music teacher, whose vocals class was among the most popular in school. Big Hutch was proudest of the fact that nearly every boy in the school had taken it and joined his chorus.

"I showed them music wasn't for pansies," he said proudly.

Now he played video poker late into the night—for sport, not money—and awoke early to help his wife, also named Pam, look after Brock's two youngest children, three-year-old Camryn and one-year-old Parker. Big Hutch earned his afternoon nap, and when he sauntered into the football offices from his silver Cadillac Coupe de Ville, he looked like a retiree who'd already had an absolutely wonderful day and knew that the best part was still ahead.

Classes were not starting until Wednesday, two days from now, but Mike Rogers, Tim Wilson, and Brock Hutchinson came in later than usual, looking haggard after a full day of faculty meetings.

"What did you do today?" Big Hutch asked his son.

"Mostly, thought about football," answered Little Hutch.

Coach Barta and Big Hutch understood Brock's anticipation. This was the first season in four years that the five coaches in this room did not know for dead sure that they had the best team in 2A. Hell, in all of Kansas. Only four of the current seniors had played meaningful minutes the year before. They had no idea who was going to replace Joe Windscheffel, who had started at quarterback for the past three years and now was at Pittsburg State on scholarship. Two seniors were vying for the job: Travis Rempe, Trevor's twin, who was an athletic 175-pounder with a strong arm, and Ethan Eastes, who was a slight 150-pounder who took care of the ball and made better decisions.

"They were all Black Shirts last year," Little Hutch offered, referring to the Redmen's second team, which donned black vests in practice. "And the Black Shirts hit us harder at practice every day than any team we faced on Fridays."

"You'd think they learned something getting killed every day for the last couple years by Kirk and Joe and Braden," said Big Hutch.

Suddenly, a shadow was cast in the coaches' office, and a hulking figure loomed in the doorway. It was Justin Nixon, a senior, who stood six feet tall and appeared to be at least four feet wide. He had a full, cherubic face that was now flashing a sleepy smile at Big Hutch.

"Coach," he said, extending a hand that looked a little bigger than a catcher's mitt.

"Big Nix," said Big Hutch, pulling that big hand closer. "You ready for a memorable season?"

Justin smiled again and nodded at Coach Barta and the others.

The coaching staff was concerned about Justin Nixon, about his fitness but mostly about his temperament. He weighed 350 pounds and was as strong as, well, an ox. He had captured the state weight-lifting championship and set a record by squatting 605 pounds and benching 460 pounds. His calves measured twenty-two inches, his biceps twenty-one, and his thighs thirty-one. He was an immovable object on the Redmen line, and recruiters were starting to discover him. The coaching staff was convinced that Justin could write his own ticket to any Division I school in the nation, but they were concerned about how he had abandoned the weight room. They knew that Big Nix was a sensitive kid and was still uncomfortable about his size and the sheer power he contained.

Mike Rogers wondered if the staff had not babied Big

Nix too much. When he was a freshman, he threatened to quit a couple of times partly because he was exhausted and partly because he was not managing the steep learning curve of trying to turn a potentially powerful body into that of a football player. They let him skip some drills that he had found too difficult, and they offered encouragement rather than driving him to become tougher.

Now, Mike believed that Justin had skipped the summer sessions because he was upset that he had not been chosen by his teammates as a captain. Mike understood how that could hurt. His son, Colt, was disappointed that he had not been selected for the honor. But Colt was a junior and was certain to be named captain next year. For Justin, this was it, and he did not understand the slight.

Coach Barta thought Justin's troubles ran deeper. The Nixons were among the hardest-working people in the community and had been for generations, but none of them had gone to college and very few had even left the county. Coach Barta thought the kid was afraid to look past Smith Center.

"I'm not sure he's even ever been to Hays," Coach Barta said, referring to a town of twenty thousand that was ninety miles south of here. "I think he's got a whole lot on him, and a whole lot he doesn't understand. He doesn't have any aspirations, and that is not his fault. Right now, I think he is afraid of succeeding."

Next through the door came Joe Osburn. Coach Barta was mildly surprised to see him. Joe was a compact five foot ten, with power chiseled in his 180-pound frame. Robert Osburn, the math teacher who had replaced Coach Barta at the high school, had adopted Joe and his younger brother, Jon. They were Hispanic and handsome, with jet-black hair, dark complexions, and bright smiles that they didn't flash too often. Both boys were vague about their circumstances, but it was known that their biological parents were alive, as were other siblings, in Kansas City.

Coach Barta believed that Joe was one of the most naturally gifted players to come through Smith Center, and his only regret was that Joe and his brothers (Joel Osburn, Robert's biological son, was also on the team) had not shown up here earlier. If they had come up in the Redmen system, the coach believed, they might be tougher, more dedicated, and more polished than they were now.

Joe had also been a no-show for much of the summer weight lifting. Brock Hutchinson reached out and tried to tell him he had an opportunity to earn a scholarship to college. It didn't take, because subsequently Joe called Coach Barta and told him that he was not going to play football or any other sport. Joe explained that he wanted to move to Garden City and find work as a meatpacker.

"I got on his ass," Coach Barta recalled. "I told him that I didn't care—that we were going to win with or without him. I told him that he was throwing away a chance to go to college and play football, but that was his decision. And then I got on him more about saying he wanted to be a meatpacker."

"Where'd you get that in your head?" the coach asked Joe. "With all the things out there in this big world, that's all you want to do?"

Thinking back to their conversations, Coach Barta lifted himself from his chair and nodded at his staff. They all understood it was going to be a challenging year.

"We're not going to solve any of these problems in here," he said, walking out into the locker room.

As Coach Barta parted the freshmen sitting on the floor,

the other coaches carried their chairs out and positioned themselves around the room. Coach Barta glanced at a few notes jotted on the back of his practice schedule; it was time to lay out the rules and expectations he had for the coming season. He did not pace or stalk, and he barely raised his voice beyond his usual conversational rumble. He made sure he looked at his players on all three sides of the locker room.

"Guys, I don't have a lot of rules, and two main ones I got I expect you to follow year-round," he said, pausing. "Don't embarrass us. Don't embarrass yourself."

He repeated it slowly, turning his head across the room. "Don't embarrass us. Don't embarrass yourself," he said. "I want you to remember that I see everything, and I hear everything. We are the number-one-ranked team in Kansas and under a tremendous amount of scrutiny. Guys, understand the drinking is over. It stops right now, and so does the smoking and tobacco chewing. I saw at least one of you smoking this summer, and that is done and over."

He glanced down at his notes. All the players' eyes were front and center as if they were afraid to be caught looking around.

"Now, if you're going to miss practice, I want you to call me yourself," he said. "I don't want your brother coming in here or a teammate. You'll understand this someday when you are a parent. When a kid is supposed to be at practice, and he doesn't show up, I get worried. I wonder if he is hurt, or if something has happened to him or to his family."

Coach Barta opened his arms in gentle, "Who me?" fashion. "I'm easy to work with, guys," he assured them. "I understand football for some of you is not the most important thing in the world. I know there are going to be times you might have to miss practice. I may not always agree with why, but I'm going to let you go. We're a team. We look after one another. We got to communicate. If you guys are afraid of me, go talk to your captains. They'll come and talk to me on your behalf. We really have to communicate."

He jammed his practice schedule into his back pocket and waded a little deeper into the freshmen on the floor. They scooted and let him pass, and pirouetted to follow him to the back of the room. He did not need notes for what he was about to tell them.

"There's something that I think the older kids already know because I tell it to them every year," he said. "You guys get what you deserve by earning it on the field. I don't care if your mom or dad is on the school board. Or if you have rich parents. Or poor parents. Or if you have two parents, one parent, or no parents. You earn it on the football field. I want to make sure everyone is clear on that."

Each nodded, acknowledging that they heard him.

"By definition, guys, someone here is the best football player on the team, and by definition, someone is the worst," he said. "I know there're at least two of you in here that are disappointed that you were not voted captains. It is the time to forget about all that. What we can do now is learn to respect each other, and when we learn to respect each other, we're going to learn to like each other. When you like each other, you learn to love each other, and then we have chemistry. And that's when together we are champions."

Coach Barta let the words sink in: *respect*, *love*, and *champions*. He wanted those words linked, and it was the fundamental value that he hoped to pass on to each and every boy he had ever coached. He nodded his head once, twice, as if he was listening to an internal metronome. He

waded back into the middle of the room, making the freshmen scoot and pirouette once more. He held their attention
in silence for another couple of beats. For a moment, it appeared he had said all that he was going to.

"There *is* one more thing, guys," he said. "I've been reading some of the preseason coverage in the media, and Lord
knows, we have reporters coming in and out of here. I guess
one of them asked one of you—I can't remember which one
of you it was—about how it would feel if we lost a game
this year."

The back of every player in the room stiffened, even
those of the freshmen sitting on the floor. Fifty-five of them
wondered who in the world had spoken about the streak;
Trevor Rempe stared straight ahead and prayed no one was
looking at him. Coach Barta let his team's discomfort stew
in the stillness. He knew it was Trevor who had made the
remarks. It surprised him because Trevor was one of his
toughest kids and was a natural leader. He thought he was
seasoned, too, after starting at fullback for the Redmen last
season throughout the playoffs when injuries had decimated
the team's backfield.

Eighteen years before, Coach Barta had run into the
Rempe twins' mother, Stacy, who had the boys snug in a
double stroller. As the coach looked down upon them, he
told Stacy the pair looked like a future fullback and quarterback. Over the ensuing years, whenever they bumped into
each other, Stacy asked the coach not to retire until her boys
could make his prediction come true.

So far Coach Barta was only half-right. Trevor was his
starting fullback; Travis was battling for the quarterback
job. Right now, however, the coach decided that Trevor
needed to take one for the team. He dialed his honey bari-

tone up to a bellow and surrendered his face to the look of disdain.

"*We don't talk about winning and losing in Smith Center, Kansas,*" he said, letting the words echo in the locker room.

Trevor shriveled up on his stool, his face turned red, and his eyes shimmered with tears.

"*We talk about getting a little bit better each day, about being the best you can be, about being a team. When we do those things, winning and losing takes care of itself.*"

# 3

You ask anyone in western Kansas, and they'll tell you that they can recognize a Smith Center kid.

—Morse Boucher, August 22, 2008

The Redmen were in pads after only two days of training camp, and with the familiar armor came a greater intensity from the players and a steady stream of onlookers. One of the luxuries Coach Barta enjoyed was not having to teach his players the precepts of the Redmen's offense or defense. By the time they came to two-a-days as freshmen, they were already deeply indoctrinated to Redmen football.

At the moment, that instruction was taking place on the adjacent practice field, where Darren Sasse was teaching seventh and eighth graders the Barta-Bone offense. Right now he was telling the midget quarterbacks how to pivot from beneath center and hand the ball off to their running backs.

"Step to six o'clock," he said. "*T* the toe, reach and ride the fullback."

Darren had also played here and had the perfect temperament for teaching twelve- and thirteen-year-olds a playbook that was far more complicated than the textbooks they were reading in school. He was extremely patient with the boys who wobbled under the weight of their helmets and pads, and got their feet tangled up so often during agility drills that it was nothing to see seven or eight of them in a pile on the rope sled. Most of the time, the junior high boys looked like they were playing dress-up for Halloween.

Like Mike Rogers, Brock Hutchinson, and Tim Wilson, Darren had discovered his calling for education and coaching at Smith Center High School under Coach Barta and Big Hutch. After graduating in 1991, Darren went to Bethany College, where he played guard and graduated with a bachelor's degree in elementary education. Coach Barta and his staff jokingly referred to him as the Redmen's first graduate assistant because he helped coach two-a-day practices each summer when he was in college. Darren had even found a copy of *Modern Belly T Football*, a book written by A. Allen Black and published in 1972, which Coach Barta had devoured and borrowed from in adapting the Redmen offense.

The return of Darren and the rest of the coaching staff was a boon for the football program and for the school district and the community at large. Four of the coaches had married teachers and were raising families here. The coaches and their wives accounted for roughly 18 percent of the district's forty-four-member faculty, and together they had eleven children either in school or heading there. Darren's record as a junior high coach was an accomplished 44–19, but it hardly began to measure the impact that he had had on Smith Center football. He was the one who continued to teach the junior high linemen, for example, to "step hole side, get your head to hole side, and turn your butt to the hole."

This means that if I am the left tackle and the running

back is running to the hole on my left, my first step is with my left foot. As I engage my defensive man, I want to try and have my head to the left side of him; if my head is between him and the ball carrier, it is harder for him to get rid of me and make the tackle. I then want to turn my butt to the left (hole side) so as to put myself between the defense and the ball carrier. Darren explained, in terms the boys could understand, the intricacies of the system that they would be playing for the next six years. Coach Barta and the high school staff took matters from there, and the results spoke for themselves.

Along with the system and the former players returning here to help teach it, hitting hard and being tough were the hallmarks of Smith Center football.

"Who hits harder?" Brock would call out frequently throughout practice.

"Nobody!" was the answer loud and in unison.

The coaching staff paid more than lip service to the notion, especially in training camp, where twice a day the players paired up in drills called "Okie," "Buffalo," or "K-State," euphemisms for the one-on-one, two-on-one, or three-on-two explosions of violence. The players "oohed" and "aahed" at the crash of shoulder pads and percussion of helmet-to-helmet collisions. Coach Barta knew it was an old-school approach, and that many high school teams at the top of the national rankings did not hit at all except on game day. He also knew that most of those schools were suburban juggernauts with hundreds of boys to cull for athletes, and with parents who could afford to send their sons to summer football camps at major colleges. Here in western Kansas, even the most dedicated boys had trouble finding time to lift weights around their farm duties or their multiple summer jobs. Camps were a luxury few could afford. Besides, the kids had bought into the essence of Redmen football, which was that if you hit harder and longer each game, your opponent would eventually quit.

The philosophy of Smith Center football, and a great many other things about the town, was explained to me on the practice field sidelines over countless evenings. The return of football season was a happening, especially in the evenings when pickups circled the practice field that sits between the high school and Hubbard Stadium. Among them was Allen Shelton, the Smith County counselor, who spent most of his day prosecuting or disposing of cases such as driving while under the influence, domestic violence, or bad check writing. Allen wandered the field with a camera and a battery of lenses, indulging in his avocation as an accomplished photographer. He spent much of his time in the county courthouse, which in the quirky urban planning of small towns formed one point of a compact triangle with the grain elevator and Smith Center's elementary school. It was jarring to see the razor-wired exercise yard of the county jail jut up to the front door of the school. The unsightly fence was installed not too long ago, the story goes, after a grade schooler was razzed for talking at recess to his father, who was a frequent guest of the county.

Allen had moved to Smith Center in 2004, after practicing law throughout western Kansas, and at the age of sixty-three he was still proud that this was a region where doors were usually unlocked and keys were left in the ignition. But neither he nor the five-member Smith County sheriff's office had its head in the sand when it came to the threat methamphetamines had brought to rural America. They had discovered labs in abandoned farmhouses and recognized the rotted teeth and corroded skin of of addicts among a handful of Smith County's residents. They also saw the number of juvenile abuse cases rise, and continued to make busts throughout the county. So far it had been a nuisance rather than an epidemic.

Earlier in the week, however, Allen and the rest of the town were served a reminder of how innocence can be quickly shattered. A career criminal already in jail had been charged with the murder and robbery of a man in Osborne County, less than twenty miles away. It was the first murder in Osborne County in fifteen years and had been followed closely in the news throughout western Kansas.

The arrest was stripped across the *Smith County Pioneer*, which was owned and edited by Jack Krier. He was at the Redmen's practice, too, a camera dangling from his neck and a notebook jammed in his back pocket. Jack was sixty-eight years old and vibrated with energy, a trait that comes in handy when you're the driving force behind a small weekly newspaper chain. He had been newspapering for more than fifty years and now co-owned twenty-six weeklies in Kansas, Missouri, and Nebraska. Jack sold ads, took pictures, and was the editorial voice of the *Smith County Pioneer* and most of his other papers. He proudly proclaimed himself "right of Attila the Hun," and his columns of late championed all things Sarah Palin and ridiculed the folly of my colleagues in the "mainstream media," especially our soft spot for "socialists" like Barack Obama. He did not hold me responsible for their foolishness, however, and we were friends. Like his readers, Jack had a genuine passion for high school sports, and the best part of his job was coming to the Redmen's practices and watching Coach Barta put the boys through their paces and visiting with whoever else roamed the practice field. Jack's office was right next to Allen's, and it was clear they engaged in a running dialogue.

They treated Coach Barta and the Redmen's success as a great mystery. They knew the man and admired him greatly, but they had a hard time getting past his easygoing nature, sifting through his coaching clichés, and being able to ascribe to him some sort of genius. They both attested that none of his players had turned up on the police blotter, and credited him with making Friday nights in the fall the most important on the county's calendar.

Jack was in the tougher position of the two because he had to build stories around the coach's proclamations, which rarely veered from two familiar themes.

"We respect every opponent and fear no one" was a favorite pregame refrain that I had already heard the coach tell four different reporters in the past week.

"I thought they played real hard," he'd say of his opponents after each game, no matter whether the Redmen had beaten them by two points or sixty.

Jack had been hearing the same phrases for four years, and he and Allen both had hoped that I might discover how exactly Coach Barta and his staff had taken undersized kids and turned them into overachievers year after year. The topic today, however, was 350-pound Justin Nixon and his impending recruiting trip to Kansas State.

Justin, too, spent a great deal of practice on the sidelines. For the past two years, he had been held out of the Redmen's hitting drills after he proved detrimental to his teammates' health. Twice in four years the coaches had let Big Nix participate in full-on contact. As a sophomore, he broke a teammate's leg, and last year he crushed the ankle and ended the season of one of the team's key seniors, Jared

Hayes. No one had felt worse about it than Justin, who was as soft-spoken as he was physically imposing. One of the most awe-inspiring sights of the summer for me was Justin wielding a Weed Eater in one hand as if it were a feather-weighted jump rope as he pushed a lawn mower with the other hand. He covered the ground with the efficiency of a combine and rolled through the yard as if he were on wheels. He operated a prolific lawn business, and it was just one of his many enterprises. He also worked at Myers Hardware in town, helped one of his four older brothers at a nursing home, and with his younger brother, Josh, a 250-pound sophomore, often cleaned up and closed the Pizza Hut at night.

Justin's father, Joe Nixon, had passed on this work ethic as well as the power gene to his second-youngest son. Joe always worked multiple jobs over the course of three marriages and raising a family of boys who ranged in age from sixteen to forty-two. Like Justin, Joe was powerfully compact—barely five feet, ten inches—and light on his feet. When the Mini-Max food warehouse in town was still open, folks marveled at how Joe balanced one-hundred-pound sacks of potatoes on either shoulder and then tossed them into the trucks like beanbags. He had since had quadruple-bypass open-heart surgery but now was back at work at the county water department.

Justin was concerned about his father's health, as well as his own ballooning weight. Last spring, as school was winding down, he suffered debilitating headaches, which led to a battery of medical tests and concern about his blood pressure. Justin also had trouble with his vision, which doctors speculated may have caused his discomfort. They fitted him with glasses, taught him about nutrition, and ordered him off sodas, which he drank by the gallon, pushing his weight close to 380 pounds and keeping him chronically dehydrated.

Justin was, indeed, bruised about not having been voted a captain. Over the summer, Marshall McCall and Colt Rogers had made many futile trips to Myers Hardware to try to lure Justin back to the weight room. The pair followed him down the aisles, telling him how important he was to the Redmen, and that he was still a team leader even if he had not been voted a captain. Justin listened impassively. He had started at left offensive tackle since he was a sophomore and had been the only junior treated as an equal by last year's senior class. They saw his talent, felt his power, and did not mind that he was a quiet kid. Why hadn't his fellow seniors recognized how much he gave to the team?

Justin did not understand why everyone was making such a big deal about his staying away from the weight room. He was trying to manage his own weight. All summer Justin had fought his prodigious appetite, replacing the sodas with two gallons of water, a quart of orange juice, and a gallon and a half of milk each day. He no longer was getting dehydrated, and with the help of his arduous work schedule, he had shed thirty pounds over the summer.

He was eager to share that progress with the coaching staff at Kansas State, where he was invited the coming weekend, along with some other recruits, for the Wildcats' opening game against North Texas State. Justin was beginning to understand the possibilities before him. A scholarship to play big-time football was in reach, and so was the prospect of becoming the first Nixon to graduate from college. He was a solid B student who wrestled down his schoolwork, albeit not without a struggle.

Justin was getting help with his study habits at the high school, learning how to organize his homework into digestible blocks of time. Losing the weight over the summer had been just the kind of victory he needed to boost his confidence.

As a further sign of his commitment, Justin vowed not to shave until the season was over to demonstrate that he was focused on running down what he knew was a once-in-a-lifetime opportunity. It was a lot to put on a seventeen-year-old, but Justin was perhaps better prepared than most thought. He was surrounded by a family that had embraced hard work, but not at the cost of their dreams. They just dreamed smaller.

"I'm a little scared," Justin confessed. "But I think it's in a good way. I've watched how hard my dad worked to keep us all fed and in clothes. My brothers work hard, too. None of them had the opportunity I have. It's not going to be easy. I know when you get to college, football is a full-time job, but it can't be any harder than what I've watched my family do. They want me to be a college graduate."

———

The following Saturday morning I was in the office talking to Coach Barta when Trevor, Travis, and Marshall excitedly rushed inside. They had seen a red Toyota Rav-4 in the parking lot with Oklahoma plates. "Is there an Oklahoma coach here?" asked Marshall, breathlessly.

When I told them that the vehicle belonged to me, disappointment washed over their faces. They had been hoping against hope that University of Oklahoma coach Bob Stoops had dispatched an assistant to scout and possibly sign one of the Redmen. This notion was not so far-fetched; the

Sooners had already gotten a verbal commitment from Marshall Musil, a running back who played for tiny La Crosse near Hays, Kansas. They knew Marshall Musil. They had been part of the team that had trounced Musil and the Leopards, 46–0, two years ago in the playoffs. Last spring, Marshall McCall was a member of the 400-meter relay team that had bested Musil and his teammates at the regional tournament in what was considered an upset.

They were not exactly jealous of Musil, and they liked him well enough. It was just that he had achieved the kind of recognition that they had not. They had beaten him convincingly on the football field and on the track, but he was going to play football on a full scholarship at one of the nation's preeminent programs while they were just hoping to extend their football careers at the junior college or small college level.

The long-promised Kansas heat showed up that morning, and the Redmen practiced sluggishly. Now they knelt around a pickup truck parked near the locker room with twenty-five watermelons in its bed.

Morse Boucher had brought them, as he had done every preseason for twenty-five years now. Morse's boys Mike and Jay had played here decades ago, and his son Doug, who helped with the team's strength program, was among the coaches who observed the game from the press box on game days. Morse and his wife, Lucille, had been among the first to welcome Roger and Pam Barta to town, and they had supported the Redmen ever since.

Morse worked the first-down chains at home games and attended most of the team's practices. He was making up for lost time. When his boys played for Coach Barta, he was too busy working and did not have the luxury to come to practice.

"I wish I could have," he said. "Because what goes on up here at school is the thing we do best in Smith Center. We raise kids to work hard and take care of each other. We teach it at home and in the classrooms, and right here on the practice field."

Morse had run the Mini-Max warehouse until it closed in the mid-1990s and sent eighty-five people looking for jobs, including Justin Nixon's father, Joe. Many of Morse's former employees had to move to Topeka or Kansas City for jobs. Morse himself stayed on as a regional produce manager for Boogart's, a long-gone grocery store chain, traveling through Kansas until he retired in 1998. He witnessed firsthand the difficulty Smith Center had in keeping businesses. The Redmen, however, had sustained the town in good times as well as the not-so-good-times the town was currently undergoing.

"I've seen businesses come and go around here," he said, "but the one thing we've always been able to count on is our boys. It's more than just winning; they come out of here with a work ethic and a sense of caring for each other.

"I know that's what I'm proudest of," he went on. "They are the town's ambassadors. They are tough and polite and want to succeed. You ask anyone in western Kansas, and they'll tell you that they can recognize a Smith Center kid."

———

Coach Barta's approach to football may have been old school, but he was decidedly New Age in his teaching methods. He organized his locker room into a metaphor for a journey, as the freshmen were assigned lockers on the east wall of the building and the seniors on the west. The sophomores and juniors were grouped in between to the south.

The goal was to work your way around the room over four years. Two-a-days were winding down, and Coach Barta knew he had a tired team. When Marshall McCall returned home in the evening, he was so sore and so beaten down that he barely managed to eat supper before heading straight for bed.

Coach Barta sat alone in a chair, his arms crossed atop his stomach at the north end of the locker room, where he called practice into session each day with a meeting. These gatherings only tangentially had anything to do with football. The start of school was approaching, and it was time to remind his team that life was about much more than football.

Marshall and the other captains had been to see him the night before asking that practice today be moved up to 3:00 p.m. so they could attend a back-to-school dance. Living without girls already was harder than it sounded. Marshall explained to the coach that this was the only dance of the fall the players thought they would be able to attend; the others were after home football games when the Redmen sometimes were slow out of the locker room and always too sore to dance.

Coach Barta did not mind. He was encouraged that the seniors had taken the initiative to ask for a special consideration. This group's growth was going to be measured in baby steps.

"Guys, we're in here a little earlier than I wanted to be so you can go the dance," Coach Barta said, calling the meeting to order. "I went along with this, so I expect you to bust your tails out here this afternoon. Now, I want to take a minute to talk about first impressions. Young'uns, you really need to listen to this. We've had reporters in here, talking to some of the older guys, and as far as I can tell, everyone has handled themselves real well.

"Like it or not, people are going to judge you on how you present yourself when they meet you. It's real important for you to show up on your dates tonight dressed properly.

"You look the adults in the eye when you shake their hands, and you say, 'yes sir,' and 'no sir,' when they ask you a question. And guys, you treat your dates like the ladies that they are, and do what a good man does. Remember they are somebody's daughters and someday they are going to be somebody's momma—so respect them.

"Coach Hutch, what you got?"

It was Coach Barta's cue for the rest of his staff to either build on his short homily or take the discussion in another direction. The order was determined by seniority and never changed: Big Hutch, Mike Rogers, Little Hutch, and Tim Wilson.

Their speaking styles were as different as they were. Big Hutch was wry, irreverent, and elicited the most laughs. Mike Rogers was sober and conscientious. He also had his son, Colt, in the room and spoke from the perspective of a parent. Little Hutch was emotional, fiery, and the one most likely to let loose an expletive. Tim Wilson was perhaps the most articulate and spoke in complete paragraphs and with forethought. Any of them could have been a head coach somewhere else, but they all had chosen to stay in their hometown and try to duplicate their childhoods for their own children. Each was comfortable with this decision. All were comfortable with one another.

Over the course of the season, the meetings were my favorite part of the day, as each coach riffed off the others like a jazz combo, delivering what were basically various keys of

Coach Barta's "do the right thing" message to a group of young men mostly eager to hear it.

The senior class especially hung on their coaches' words. They may have lacked confidence, but they were hungry to find a way to become better. Three of the captains (Trenton Terrill, Kris Lehmann, and Marshall McCall) were honor students, and the fourth (Trevor Rempe) was the perennial lead in the school play and a member of the high school's elite vocal group, the Chansonaires.

The seniors wanted desperately to improve, and if that meant trying to pick the pearls of wisdom from their coaches at team meetings, so be it. In fact, they were leaving no stone unturned when it came to building a cohesive team to keep the winning streak intact.

Marshall built a clubhouse behind his house much like the one Joe Windscheffel had provided for his class. His father, Shane, bought a prefabricated shed and, with the help of other fathers of seniors, tricked it out with electricity and cable.

Shane told everyone that he would convert the clubhouse to a workshop after Marshall graduated. It was merely a cover story. Shane wanted his son and his teammates to have every opportunity to succeed. He had played defensive back at Washburn University and had the remarkable memory of trying to defend against Mississippi Valley State's wide receiver Jerry Rice, a future pro football Hall of Famer who ran past him time and again.

"It was like he could catch BBs in the dark," Shane said of the experience.

Washburn was a long way from big-time college football, but he had earned a scholarship there and went on to get a law degree at the school. It was a Washburn alumnus who had called Shane to the attention of the football coach there. The man, a local farm implement dealer, had even given Shane five hundred dollars a semester to help offset his expenses.

Still, college football felt like a job to Shane. His fonder memories were of playing high school football for Stockton, a town of 1,500 fifty-two miles southwest of Smith Center. He understood the innocence of high school football, of playing for your friends and for the pride of your town, and how it gave you options beyond your small town. The highs were higher and the lows lower in high school, and they still are.

Even now, twenty-five years later, Coach Barta had heard that Shane was still angry about a remark he had made when the Redmen played the Stockton Tigers. Anything said in the visiting locker room at Stockton could be heard through the vents of the Tigers' dressing area. Coach Barta, hoping to fire up his team, called out the Stockton running back for being soft and afraid of being hit. He was talking about Shane McCall, and Shane had heard him. Some friends of his in town had told Coach Barta that Shane still had not let it go.

Shane, and most of the fathers of seniors, were likewise hearing doubts aired about their sons. Shane was a trust officer and did legal work at the People's Bank in town, an epicenter of the town talk. Like any parent, he wanted Marshall to succeed. And as someone who knew how a successful senior season in high school football could confer a lifetime of respect on you in your hometown, he was happy to front the costs for the clubhouse. Three other fathers—John Terrill, Trenton's dad; Dave Mace, whose son, Kalen, started at end; and Bill Rempe, the father of Trevor and Travis—helped Shane put it together and hoped for the best.

Marshall was proud of the clubhouse. He lined it with carpet, solicited couches from neighbors, and put in a refrigerator. He hung a big-screen television that was wired for PlayStation 2 and Nintendo and, as a nod to last year's seniors, found a Ping-Pong table.

"We're a lot more high-tech than Joe's," he told me proudly.

On my first visit, however, the first thing Marshall wanted me to see was his father's team photo from his senior year at Washburn. He and Shane were close. They followed Kansas State together and each year took an all-boys road trip with the Maces, the Terrills, and the Rempes to one of the Wildcats' away games.

"I owe him a lot," Marshall said, not all that sheepishly.

———

There was at least one constituency in Smith Center that was not fretting over the upcoming Redmen season: the mothers of the seniors. They believed unconditionally in their boys. They let them know it one night at a hot dog dinner and preseason meeting of the Red Caps, the athletic booster group. Coach Barta had just finished his annual preseason welcome to the parents, reminded them that he was the coach and their sons would earn their playing time on the field, and thanked them in advance for respecting his decisions. Even after thirty years and a record of excellence that someday was going to put him in the state of Kansas's coaching Hall of Fame, he knew that inoculating yourself from town backbiting was good business.

He also thanked the parents for their support, especially for preparing the pre- and postgame meals that he believed were vital to growing boys. Lyna Mace rose to explain the program to the newer parents, how for road games they would make sack lunches for the players to eat on the bus and provide minipizzas from Pizza Hut for the ride home. For home games they would prepare a lasagna dinner, complete with garlic bread and salad, which they would serve in the cafeteria after school let out.

"We've broken down the costs, and we're asking each of you for sixty-five dollars for the season, which is five dollars per game for all thirteen," she said.

The dads in the audience looked stricken. The players, who were sitting on the edge of the stage, were delighted and grinned appreciatively at the faux pas. Thirteen games meant that Lyna had just penciled them all the way through an eight-game regular season, the playoffs, and into the state championship game. The coaches may not allow the players to talk about wins and losses, but at least their mothers believed that they possessed everything they needed to be champions.

# 4

We have two very big things going for us, and the first is Roger. It's not just the winning. It's his philosophy— it's inclusive. He gets the whole town invested. The other thing is that people around here really, really like football.

—Greg Koelsch, August 30, 2008

Bob Rethorst, our real estate agent, had been correct, and a suitable house had turned up south of the railroad tracks and about a hundred yards from the grain elevator. It did not take long for three-year-old Jack Drape to be decitified. It began with a single grasshopper, a species of insect that he had never seen on the concrete playgrounds of New York. It led to a bug kit, complete with net and magnifying glass, and led to endless excursions into the grass. He crouched down on his haunches and marveled at the crickets and slugs, who blew his tiny mind daily.

The grain elevator became "*Our grain elevator, Dad!*" Whenever a train whistled, we ran to the sidewalk to watch it groan back and forth as its cars were filled with wheat or soybeans or milo. And our two-bedroom home at 509 South Main Street became the jumping-off point for bedtime stories that always began the same.

*Once upon a time, there was a little boy named Jack*
*Who lived beneath a grain elevator,*
*Across from the railroad tracks*
*In a little yellow house,*
*With a big red car in the driveway,*
*And a little blue scooter on the front step . . .*

They usually ended the same way as well—with the grass-hopper introducing my son to a farmer who explained how the wheat he grew here in Smith County ended up in the Lucky Charms cereal that boys like Jack in New York City ate.

Jack had come here as a Manhattan-dwelling toddler who spent too much time in his stroller, weaving in and out of pedestrian traffic en route to the grocery store or playground. Now his stroller remained in the back of our rental car, as it would for our entire stay, and he was turning into a little boy.

He proudly put his Wall-E backpack over his shoulder and ran to the car to be taken to preschool classes at the First St. John's Lutheran Church in Kensington, fifteen miles west on Highway 36. There he learned how to trace, cut out, and remember his alphabet for a fraction of what it costs for preschool in New York City. In the afternoon, Jack came with me to football practice, where he had full run of the place.

He filled ice bags for injuries the players did not have, and he burrowed deep in the equipment room hiding from the team managers in games of hide-and-seek. Jack called them the "water boys," and Brody Frieling, L. T. Meitler, Gavin Overmiller, Beau Drake—all eleven years old—and nine-year-old Colton Hutchinson were the latest in a long line of a proud tradition. Just like the Rempe twins, Trenton Terrill, and Colt Rogers before them, they were preparing to be Redmen by picking up towels and handing out water as grade schoolers. Once practice started, Jack and the managers broke into teams and ran plays alongside the old white panel milk truck that hauled water and equipment the two hundred yards between the football complex and the practice field. I'd catch glimpses of Jack hugging the football with both hands as the water boys purposely missed tackling him as he ran. I'd break into a smile that matched his as he giggled en route to an imaginary goal line. Jack didn't like the sunflower seeds that the water boys chewed, but he liked burying a handful of them in the dirt, squirting them with a water bottle, and telling me the yellow and black flowers would sprout by practice tomorrow.

For the first time in his short life, Jack knew what he wanted to be when he grew up: a football-playing farmer.

Dad and Mom also warmed up to the details of rural small-town living. I raised my right index finger from the steering wheel by way of greeting as I passed other vehicles. I got used to the funeral notices that would be stacked on the counter of the Pizza Hut, the pharmacy, and the grocery store. I asked after the farmers, who drank coffee and killed time at the Formica-topped tables in the convenience stores along Highway 36. I understood that everyone had a rainfall gauge and wanted to compare notes with their neighbors after any downpour. I waited patiently in checkout lines while folks actually wrote checks for their purchases without having to produce identification.

There was no hiding in Smith Center, nor did we want to. We were asked to speak at the Chamber of Commerce, the Rotary and Kiwanis clubs, the retirement village, and the high school. We were invited to dinner and made friends. Best of all, we learned about things absolutely foreign to us, such as farming and hunting. We also were relearning some things we had both been taught as children of the Midwest by our own families: that raising children takes love, patience, and hard work, and that being surrounded by a community committed to those values makes the job a whole lot easier.

We were frequently asked what it was like to come from New York City to a small farm town. There are a zillion answers and they come in many shades, but the most palpable difference was in population and geography. Smith County is nine hundred square miles and probably contains as many windmills as people. New York City is one-third of its size physically and is home to more than eight million people. About as many people live on my block on the East Side of Manhattan as in the whole town of Smith Center.

Our senses were reminded constantly of the differences. Mary held audiences spellbound with her tale of her first day in Smith Center. She had quit her job selling advertising and for the first time in more than twenty years did not have a career. She was accustomed to blowing out of her apartment in a sprint in the morning and living at New York's breakneck speed throughout the day. There were subways to pile into and crowds to part and lines to stand in. On her first day in Smith Center, however, she and Jack managed to walk through town and not see a single soul on the sidewalk. When they arrived at Wagner Park, they discovered they had it all to themselves.

"Where are all the people?" she said first to Jack that day

and later to our audiences. For a moment, a scary one, she confessed that she wondered what she had done.

It was startling that crossing town here took just a minute and a half by car, and the only time we came to a stop was at the four-way on Court Street. When we heard sirens here, we did not tune them out as in New York. Our hearts sank because they signaled that somebody we knew had taken ill or had been in an accident or was in some kind of trouble. Instead of the lights that flickered and the people that bustled around the clock in New York, more than half the day here could be spent in complete darkness—save for a sky full of stars that twinkled to the rhythm of the ever-blowing wind.

Smith Center is an aging community; more than 5 percent of the people in the county are at least eighty-five years old, the highest proportion of any county in the United States, and a quarter of the county's 4,500 residents are above the age of sixty-five.

It meant that Smith Center was home to a lot of folks with a lot of wisdom, and we wanted to soak up its charms and eccentricities. One place that offered plenty of both was the Second Cup Café on Main Street. It was headquarters for one of Smith Center's most eclectic groups. They called themselves the "As the Bladder Fills Club," and they gathered at the center table from eight to nine each morning to discuss the important matters of the day. They were at once the town's institutional memory, depository of wit and wisdom, and Greek chorus.

Jack Benn and his wife, Arlene, had made sure we knew our way around the Second Cup Café as well as the rest of town. They had showed up on our doorstep almost as soon as we came to town with the tastiest tomatoes and cucumbers that they pulled from their garden. Jack was a retired soil conservation officer for the U.S. Department of Agriculture. He had overseen the terracing of much of the farmland that in turn allowed the area to prosper. He knew every kind of grass and tree on these prairies. He also was an accomplished angler and had taught hunting safety to two generations of the town's boys. Arlene had also worked for the USDA, and now was a pie maker without peer and the hostess of fish frys that she made look effortless and which brought together people from every walk of life in town.

During football season, Jack and Arlene were devoted Redmen fans. Their son, Dirk, had played on Coach Barta's first Smith Center team in 1978, and the Benns had not missed a game in thirty years, even though Jack had had his bladder removed four years earlier after a bout of cancer, which made long travel difficult. They wore red, sat on their official Redmen blanket, and drove to all four corners of the state in every kind of weather.

The core group of the As the Bladder Fills Club were all retired except for Dr. Bill Grimes, a seventy-nine-year-old dentist. Stan Hooper, eighty, had managed railroad terminals in central Kansas. Dick Stroup, sixty-seven, had run the furniture store, which like the railroad was long gone. Ivan Burgess, eighty-four, had manned the post office. Bruce Miles, sixty-seven, was a retired high school principal from Colorado who had bought the Ingleboro Mansion in 2000 and, along with his wife, Bobbi, turned it into a bed-and-breakfast. There was no requirement for membership in the club other than showing up. Some mornings up to a half-dozen others would pull up a chair for some breakfast and banter. It was not a place for the humorless, politically correct, or faint of heart. Everyone owned a needle, wore a smile, and wielded both like a sword and shield.

When John Boden, who ran the city's ten-hole golf course—which allowed a different configuration for a front nine and back nine—lamented that driving the fifteen miles to and from Kensington to coach girls' volleyball meant that he was actually making only ninety-nine cents a day, Stroup didn't miss a beat.

"I always thought you were overpaid," he said.

When John McDowell, a seventy-two-year-old farmer who now helped his son-in-law cut meat at Ladow's Market in nearby Lebanon, bemoaned the fact he was running out of space in the family plot up the Hill at the cemetery, Jack Benn suggested he get himself cremated.

"All you'd need is a posthole digger," Jack went on in his mellifluous deadpan delivery. "I'd be happy as a puppy with a belly full of pee and a mile of fence post to bury you myself. In fact, I'd dig that hole nice and deep and get you halfway to where you're going anyway."

When Ivan Burgess spiked a fever and was hospitalized overnight, the As the Bladder Fills crew had a field day. "I heard it was because he had an erection that lasted more than four hours," said Stan Hooper.

"I think he's getting his vasectomy reversed," offered Dick Stroup.

Rarely did the outside world penetrate the morning conversation. It mattered little to anyone here that Barack Obama's mother and grandparents were from Kansas. These were as rock-ribbed Republican folk as you could find.

Sure, they knew that Obama was popular, but still most thought his was a long-shot candidacy. Why wouldn't they? Not a single television advertisement for Obama or

Republican John McCain aired in the months before the election.

The Beijing Olympics also were in full swing, but they barely registered at the Second Cup Café. When they did, it was as a punch line.

"Boy, I'm getting old," Ivan Burgess proclaimed one morning. "I was watching sand volleyball, and those girls didn't have enough on to cover a gnat's navel. Embarrassed me. Last time I saw 'em doing anything like that they were wearing bloomers."

No, the conversation here revolved around the comings and goings of the people who inhabited the 1.2 square miles of town and the issues facing Smith County. The members of the As the Bladder Fills Club told me that if I wanted to know what was going on in town, I could either (a) go to Pooches, the town's one bar, on Friday night, (b) come to the Second Cup Café for breakfast on Saturday mornings, or (c) go to services on Sunday morning at one of the town's eleven churches.

The Second Cup Café had the added value of being the unofficial office of the *Echo*, which Ivan Burgess published each Saturday. Ivan spent his week gathering all the news that was fit to print about Smith Center, as well some musings and anecdotes that were not fit to print at all but were a lot of fun to read. Grammar in the *Echo* was sometimes fractured and the spelling could be challenging, but Ivan painted a picture of the week's news that was as complete as an almanac and picaresque as an adventure novel.

The *Echo* had started in 1962 on a single sheet that Ivan used to send to school with his third-grade son, Kelly, who sold it to his teachers for a dime and kept the money. Now Kelly Burgess was fifty-four and the principal of Smith Center's elementary school. Ivan parlayed this report into a column called "The Coffee Break" for the *Smith County Pioneer*, the local weekly, but after a couple of years Ivan had competition from an English teacher at the high school who had started a competing paper called the *Heartland Herald Echo*. When it went belly up, Ivan decided to go back to guerrilla publishing. He gave the *Echo* a tag line: THE PEOPLE'S CHOICE FOR A NEWSPAPER VOICE IN THE HEART OF THE HEARTLAND EMPIRE. He called his enterprise Last Legs Publishing and cranked out close to three thousand words a week with dot-dot-dots separating column items that combined the saucy cadence of Walter Winchell with the down-home wisdom of Will Rogers. He sold two hundred or so copies each week for a quarter, and you could find the *Echo* in markets and cafés in all four corners of the county. There were also at least fifty people on his e-mail list.

"The reason I write the *Echo* is because I have no talent," he claimed. "I can't repair a car. I can't build a house. I can't wire a home. I can't farm. I can't sing or dance. I can't do anything. So what's left? I try to write, and I am terrible at that. People in Smith Center consider me nothing more or less than a harmless buffoon."

What Ivan really was, was a newsman. He had adopted the voice and genre of what the *Smith County Pioneer* once called its "country correspondents," who contributed news from their communities. Nothing was too insignificant, whether it be the week's rainfall amounts or who bought the county's first television set. Ivan carried on this tradition. The *Echo* had clout, too. Whenever the Rotary Club or the Chamber of Commerce or the school district wanted to turn out a crowd, they printed up an announcement for the event or fund-raiser and made sure Ivan inserted it inside the *Echo*.

There was no doubt Ivan was a character, and he often poked fun at himself in the pages of the *Echo*. "When I was in high school I had deceptive speed," he wrote. "I was actually slower than I looked." Or: "One time we was a playing, Beloit, I think it was, but it was somebody with a mean linebacker. Coach put me in the game and I scared the big linebacker to death. He thought he had killed me."

Mostly Ivan reminded folks that while the economic charts might rank Smith County among the poorest in Kansas, the good people here knew better. They knew the town's schools were far more than the county's biggest employer. They were Smith Center's heart and soul, and he reported on them with gusto.

Ivan Burgess was part of the reason that the stands were just as full for the girls' volleyball games as they were for the football team on Friday nights. But there was no denying that life in town always got a little more exciting when football season rolled around. Smith Center folks would soon be rolling their blankets out on aluminum stands across western Kansas and tuning in to KQMA-FM for its broadcasts of Redmen football. They would be escaping the tedium of retirement or the hard work of farming, and cheering on sons and grandsons, nephews and grandnephews. It was about being there for "our boys," in whom they had invested their love, patience, and hard work for generations.

———

On Saturday, August 30, we were on our way to Manhattan, Kansas, to see Mark Simoneau get inducted into the Kansas State Ring of Honor at halftime of the Wildcats' opening game. Greg Hobelmann, Smith Center High School's athletic director, was at the wheel, and the school's principal,

Greg Koelsch, was riding shotgun. We were hardly alone; we had already passed Coach Barta and Big Hutch and a half-dozen other cars with Smith Center decals. In all, about 150 folks from town would watch the most famous Redman of them all enter K-State's Hall of Fame. He had been an All-American linebacker there and was now in his eighth year in the National Football League, playing for the New Orleans Saints.

Simoneau had gone farther in football than any other Redman, and his was the only jersey that hung in a place of honor in the Smith Center locker room. His folks had moved from town, but he came back and conducted football camps and sent back autographed gear for charity golf tournaments. In fact, Greg and Greg were making the two-and-a-half-hour trek largely to thank Simoneau for what he had done for the high school and the community. It also was the last weekend before school started, which meant it was the last days they had left when time would be their own.

Greg Hobelmann was typical of teachers in rural western Kansas: he wore many hats and had to teach himself a variety of skills. He had grown up on a farm east of here near Belleville, had earned a bachelor of music education degree from Wichita State, and had taught and coached a wide range of classes and sports, from band to girls' basketball, as well as golf and cross country.

At age forty-one, he was in his fourth year as Smith Center's athletic director, with a budget of more than $265,000 and a never-ending list of duties. Greg scheduled the games for all sports, boys and girls, seventh grade to varsity. He scheduled the buses, hired the officiating crews, and often took money at the door. Beginning four days from now, Greg would put as many as five hundred miles a week on the Suburban owned by United School District 237 and half that many on his own truck, bouncing around western Kansas with one team or another.

Greg Koelsch, the principal, was just thirty-two, and he already had his master's degree in education from Fort Hays State. Greg had followed his father, a coach and administrator for more than thirty years, into the profession. He had roofed and helped his father-in-law with the cattle as he worked his way through graduate school. Greg's older sister taught and coached in McPherson, Kansas; his younger brother was at Bethany College studying to be a history teacher and coach somewhere in the state.

"It's the family business," he explained, smiling.

Both men had young families of their own but had found enough time over the summer to burn up the golf courses. And both were eager for school to start. It was the football season, they admitted, that made their reentry easier; the hallways were happier during the week, and the football games gave the kids a destination on the weekends.

"Kids don't get in trouble because they want to be part of football," Greg Hobelmann said.

It helped that 70 percent of the boys at Smith Center High School were on the football team. The Redmen, however, also gave structure and purpose to many in the 165-member student body. There was a cheerleading squad and dance team. Various clubs worked the concession stands. Greg Hobelmann had created a student broadcast team complete with on-field cameras, soundboard, and instant replay that produced a polished telecast that aired on the local cable access channel. It was Greg Hobelmann and his team, really, that programmed Channel 17.

"We have two very big things going for us, and the first

is Roger," Greg Koelsch said. "It's not just the winning. It's his philosophy—it's inclusive. He gets the whole town invested. The other thing is that people around here really, really like football."

The people of Smith Center were, indeed, passionate enough about the Redmen specifically and football in general to wait in a miles-long line before the K-State game for an autograph from Mark Simoneau. It was a muggy afternoon, and when the session came to an end and scores of townsfolk were still a quarter of a mile from Simoneau's table, they were sweaty and disappointed, but only for a moment. Suddenly, a cluster of K-State recruits knifed through the crowd on their way to the sidelines, and in the center of them was Justin Nixon. He was wearing a Redmen T-shirt and a radiant smile as his teammates and parents applauded and shouted encouragement.

The Smith Center faithful need not have worried about missing Simoneau, either. After the game, the Smith Center contingent was gathered on the field for a group photograph. In the middle of them walked a dark-haired six-footer who was trim and strong but hardly had the look of an NFL linebacker. It was Mark Simoneau. For more than an hour, he posed for photographs, signed helmets and footballs, and spoke with every Redman, mother, father, and grandparent.

He and I had spoken on the phone the previous year, before my first trip to Smith Center. He was on his lunch break at the Saints practice complex, and usually such phone interviews are brief and perfunctory. Instead, it was Simoneau who stretched the conversation past a half hour until he finally had to return to practice. As one memory after another tumbled out of a guy who had made several million dollars playing a game he learned in Smith Center, it was clear his heart remained there as well.

"You make sure you tell Coach we talked," Simoneau told me that afternoon on the phone. "As good a coach as he is, he's a better guy. He treats people like gold. That's one special place."

Now, Mark Simoneau was showing that he meant every word he had said. He could have been celebrating K-State's victory at a fancy reception with the university's biggest donors. Instead, he was here catching up with his old neighbors and coaches. When it was time to say good-bye, Coach Barta offered a hand. Simoneau gave him a hug.

"You know I love you," the coach said.

"Me, too, Coach," Simoneau said. "You taught me a lot."

# PART TWO

# THE PLANTING

# 5

You don't want to spend time with your mommas and dads because you don't think they're very smart. In fact, you know you're a lot smarter than them.

—Roger Barta, September 3, 2008

Coach Barta did not know the guy and does not remember his name. He was in San Antonio, where the U.S. Army All-American Bowl Selection had just named him national coach of the year, and sitting around a table with coaching colleagues from around the nation, most of whom congratulated him on the honor. The coaches were curious to know how Coach Barta had turned the Redmen of rural Kansas into a national power.

Not this guy.

"He told me, 'I don't know you from Adam, but I think you're an asshole for running up the score on those guys,'" Coach Barta recalled.

The unknown coach was talking about the seventy-two points that Smith Center had put up against Plainville in the first quarter of a game the previous season. It had broken a national record set by Prescott High School of Arizona in 1925, and it was the story that had first brought Coach Barta's career accomplishments and the Redmen's current streak into the national spotlight. It was also a milestone that deeply embarrassed Coach Barta.

"We're not here to embarrass kids," he said. "We're not here to run up the score. We want our kids to play hard and get ready for the next round of the playoffs. This just sort of happened. And once it started, I didn't know what to do."

He was revisiting that game, wincing once again at what the coach in San Antonio had said because we were standing outside the Hubbard football complex waiting to board the Redmen's bus for the opening game of the 2008 season in—where else?—Plainville. As the players loaded the team's red equipment bags into the belly of the red, white, and green bus, Coach Barta wanted me to know that if he could have that game, that quarter, back and save his hometown from that humiliation, he would. He told me how he and his wife, Pam, had grown up in Plainville, a gritty little oil town, and how it was there that he was inspired to become a coach and educator. He had fallen under the spell of his American Legion baseball and high school football coach, a gruff, tireless, and generous man named Al Hargrave.

"He would haul us around and kind of raised us like his own sons," he told me. "When we were in high school, he had us coach Little League teams. When we were in college, he'd have us come back and coach American Legion.

"He was probably the first teacher who taught me that the way to make an impact with a kid was to love him and treat him with respect. It was his foundation that I built a lot of what I do on."

He had played quarterback at Plainville, but a back injury prevented him from continuing his football career in college. Instead, he went to Fort Hays State University and halfheartedly pursued a math degree. During Christmas vacation of his sophomore year, he took a job in the oil fields, hoping it might lead to a full-time job and an escape from school. It took but a single rainy day high on a derrick to send him right back.

"I about froze to death," Coach Barta said. "I looked around, and all the guys looked like they were ninety years old even though they were only in their fifties. They were missing fingers and teeth. I didn't want to do that for the rest of my life."

He returned to Fort Hays and graduated in 1967. He was teaching and coaching junior high in Atwood, Kansas, when he won a scholarship to the University of Georgia to get a master's degree in education. He hoped to land a teaching and coaching job in his hometown, so he and Pam could watch out for their parents—both sets farmers—as they raised their own family. They ended up in WaKeeney, in Trego County, Kansas, where he would spend seven years as an assistant coach. In 1978, one of his fraternity brothers from Fort Hays told him that the Smith Center job was open, but Pam wasn't keen on moving. Still, Barta wanted his own program, and he applied for the job, won it, and moved his family to Smith Center.

Smith Center and Plainville had been friendly rivals, and the Cardinals played good football, winning state championships in 1980 and 1985. When Plainville showed up at Hubbard Stadium for a state playoff game in 2007, Coach Barta was not worried that his team would be upset. He also didn't think his boys were going to put seventy-two points on the scoreboard in twelve minutes.

They wouldn't have, either, if not for one lightning strike after another of luck—the good kind for Redmen fans, the worst kind for the Cardinal faithful. The Redmen ran just fifteen offensive plays, fourteen of them runs, and seven of them went for touchdowns of forty-nine, ten, thirty-nine, twenty-three, three, twenty-nine, and sixty yards. Plainville simply could not tackle the Smith Center running backs and could not stop the Redmen from converting their two-point attempts. Coach Barta pulled his starters halfway through the massacre and sent word to his athletic director, Greg Hobelmann, that he needed to get ahold of the Kansas State High School Activities Association and ask—no, plead—for them to institute the "mercy rule." In the regular season, once a team took a lead of forty points, the clock ran continuously in an effort to limit the carnage, but this rule did not hold for playoff games. While Hobelmann was trying to reach association officials, the Cardinals kept shooting themselves in the foot: they threw an interception that was returned for a touchdown, and fumbled the ball away five times, all of which led to scores.

By the time the high school association sanctioned the running clock, the damage was already done. Coach Barta ordered his players to go down on the 5-yard line if they were about to score, and allowed his seldom-used kicker to try some field goals. When the game was over, the scoreboard read Smith Center 83, Plainville 0.

On high school Internet message boards and among some of its coaching fraternity, Coach Barta was, indeed, proclaimed an "asshole" for running up the score.

Now, ten months later, the Redmen's bus was loaded with juniors and seniors—the underclassmen trailed behind in a yellow school bus—and the 2008 football season was about to kick off. Some T-shirts on sale at the high school encapsulated what had become the annual expectation. SAME OLD STORY; NEW CHAPTER was the featured slogan.

It was a fitting epithet for how Coach Barta prepared his team year in and year out. He was a slave to habit, and it extended from his practice schedule to the pregame rituals and even to his own superstitions. For road games, he made sure his team was at the opponents' field at least two and a half hours before kickoff. He and Big Hutch were always the last two to board the bus, grabbing a sack lunch and carrying a pillow.

They sat in the front row, across the aisle from each other, and were among the first to fall asleep. Silence was the rule. The Redmen reread their scouting reports and then closed their eyes and focused on how the game might unfold and how each of them would execute. Coach Barta had taught them to visualize a victory.

"See it, feel it, believe" was the mantra.

The Redmen played in the Mid-Continent League, a seven-team football conference that ensured bus travel of anywhere from forty minutes to two hours. Once the play-offs started, the travel times would expand anywhere from two and a half to six hours. The MCL was a proud football conference and was considered the best in western Kansas. Like many high school leagues in rural America, the premium in the MCL was on proximity rather than size of schools. Norton and Phillipsburg, for example, competed in 3A, which was for schools that had up to 194 students in tenth, eleventh, and twelfth grades, while Smith Center, with 116 students, competed in 2A. The Redmen, however, were seldom outgunned and over the years had beaten plenty of 4A teams (up to 503 students). In 1985, the MCL had ten schools, and three of its members won state championships: Norton (4A), Plainville (3A), and Victoria (2A). Dwindling populations, however, had taken their toll on the league:

Norton was down to 3A, and this season Stockton and Hill City had dropped to eight-man football, the smallest classification in Kansas state football.

As the Redmen slept on the bus to Plainville, the landscape of Kansas, at once forbidding and breathtaking, passed by on Highway 36. What was once home to buffalo and Indians and homesteaders and gunslingers is now farmland and fertile hunting grounds. Below the solitary red-tailed hawk or formation of turkey buzzards, tall grasses bent and windmills turned, framing thousands upon thousands of acres of wheat, sprouting the brown-green fuzz that looks like the burned-out greens of a golf course at the end of a heavily trafficked season.

The vivid colors of summer had given way to the mechanics of growing the staple of farm life here: wheat. The winter wheat was now being planted and would continue to be into December. It would sprout before the freezing occurred and remain dormant until the soil heated up in the spring. In July it would be harvested and find its way into our diets. Soft spring wheats become all-purpose flour used in baked goods. Hard winter wheats, rich in protein and gluten, are important to yeast breads. Durum, the hardest wheat, is planted in the spring and makes pasta.

The man-made ruins are not nearly as charming or practical. T.J.'s Toys, Autos & Spas seemingly offered something for everyone but never appeared to draw a crowd. And eBay has nothing on rural Kansas, where ranch houses with caved-in roofs and rusted farm equipment in their yards tout antiques, and dusty windowed storefronts on abandoned Main Streets hold auctions. In Smith Center, it was Stortz's Auction, once the home of the Chevrolet dealership. Instead of Novas and Corvettes rolling off the showroom floor, now it was furniture, drum sets, and porcelain figurines being carted out at pennies on the dollar. All too often these auction companies hosted farm estate sales where tractors, machinery, and a way of life were sold off to the highest bidder, usually at a heartbreakingly low price.

When the bus rolled through Phillipsburg, Stockton, and finally Plainville, folks on the sidewalks turned and stared. They didn't need to see SMITH CENTER REDMEN written on its side. They knew it was Friday afternoon, and that Friday evenings around here belonged to high school football. For decades now, the Redmen had been the night's biggest stars in this part of Kansas. Roger Kelley, a farmer with a shock of white hair and leathery face who moonlighted as the Redmen's bus driver, nosed the coach into the stadium and behind a tiny concrete hut that was the visitors' locker room. He cranked open the door, got out, lit a cigarette, and watched the players pour out.

They walked directly onto the field and circled one goalpost, and then marched down to the other end of the field to do the same. It was sunny and seventy degrees outside, so they wore the gray shorts and red T-shirts. It was 4:30 p.m., and no one was there to see the procession, not even the home team, which had yet to arrive. This was part of the Redmen's pregame ritual. It didn't matter that they were far from home and on enemy ground, once the ball was kicked off they would own this field. When the lap was completed, they returned to the bus to unload their equipment.

The players filed into the tiny locker room in shifts, emerging in waves wearing their red away pants and white jerseys but carrying their helmets and shoulder pads. They had an hour yet before warm-ups, and it was time to find a place in the shade where they could stretch out, close their eyes, and envision the perfect game they intended to play in a couple of hours. This was by Coach Barta's design as well. He, too, liked to put his head on a pillow before the game in order to anticipate and envision what might happen over forty-eight minutes of football. He and Big Hutch found a place in the shade to focus.

Mike Rogers, however, was restless and remained at midfield. He was on edge for many reasons. First, Mike was a fierce competitior—he had been all his life. He was a starter for the Redmen as a junior in 1982, rushing for 2,029 yards and leading the way for Smith Center's first state football championship. He was the team's first All-State player, and the following year he had big-time college coaches knocking at his door. Mike enjoyed a couple of solid seasons at the University of Kansas but never dominated as he had in high school.

At age forty-two, Mike still had the powerful build of a running back, and he was an accomplished outdoorsman who began most mornings checking the twenty-four animal traps he set each night in hopes of catching raccoons, possums, and bobcats. He lived west of Smith Center on sixteen acres in a house that he and his father had built together from scratch. Mike had a hard time sitting still.

He was even jumpier for this opening game because his son, Colt, was expected to be a major contributor this year. Colt started at running back and safety, returned kicks, and arguably was the best all-around athlete on the team. Unfortunately, Colt possessed the genes of his petite mother, Cally, and wasn't going to come close to reaching Mike's six-foot, 240-pound frame. In fact, Colt stood just five feet three inches and weighed 135 pounds.

What Colt had inherited from his father was speed and strength, as well as an outsized confidence and stubbornness. It made for a superior competitor, but at home it was making for a handful of a teenage son. Lately, Colt had been sullen around his mother. He was pushing every day to hang out more with his friends, and even when he was home, he stayed up late talking on his cell phone to his girlfriend, Lexie. She lived in Phillipsburg, and Colt had warned her that football needed to be his first love for a couple of months. Easier said than done, apparently; Colt had been up at all hours on the telephone with her.

Finally, Mike made Colt turn over the cell phone each night at ten thirty, making their relationship even frostier. He understood immediately why: Mike was amazed how the phone rang or buzzed with text messages on his bed stand until two in the morning.

"When we were kids, you had a four-foot phone cord and your mom or dad sitting there next to you, listening in," Mike said, standing at midfield, still bewildered. "Now, with text and e-mails, kids can lead a completely independent life if you let them."

Mike had asked Brock Hutchinson to have a heart-to-heart with Colt. Brock was Colt's wrestling coach, and over hundreds of hours on the mats, he had become the older brother Colt never had. Coach Barta had seen what was going on between Mike and Colt, and he slipped the notion of appreciating your family into a team meeting without betraying the Rogerses.

"Guys, I know you're back in school, and you've had a summer where you really have felt you've grown up," he began. "Now football is here, and you sophomores and juniors especially think you know a lot about life. I try to talk about this every year because I've watched this go on for forty years now. Heck, I saw it with my own kids.

"You don't want to spend time with your mommas and dads because you don't think they're very smart. In fact, you know you're a lot smarter than them. Now, I think the seniors over here will agree with me on this because they're at the age where they think that their parents aren't so dumb after all."

He then looked over to the west wall where a few of the seniors did nod almost imperceptibly.

"And, oh, about twenty-one or so, all of you guys are going to realize that your folks knew a lot more than you ever gave them credit for," he continued. "Now I'm telling you this because I think young people need to be reminded that their moms and dads are the people who love them the most. They do things for you guys that you don't even understand yet. You will someday when you have your own kids, and it will break your heart when they fight with you.

"So, guys, listen to your parents. Spend some time with them. Tell them you love them. They care about you."

Mike was standing his ground at home, but right now he was anxious about how Colt might play tonight, and about whether he could keep a clear head coaching his son. He was having a hard time being both a father and coach. He was not a screamer or a hard guy. At practice, he spoke softly and evenly and was the most touchy-feely member of the staff. He thought nothing of putting two comforting hands on a kid's shoulders or drawing a player close for a hug. He was stoic during games, but his competitive juices boiled inside, especially when Colt carried the ball. His jaw tensed, and he leaned from one foot to another as if he were making the cuts on the field himself. The qualities that made Colt a terrific competitor were the ones that aggravated Mike the most. His son tried too hard to make big plays, hurling his small frame at piles, wildly spinning away from tacklers.

On the wrestling mat, Colt's tactics looked graceful and were effective, as he was virtually unbeatable against opponents in his own weight class. In football, his extra effort was as obvious as his size disadvantage. And sometimes it led to mistakes, like fumbling the ball. Mike knew if Colt had his druthers he'd play football in college. He also knew his son's size was going to make that improbable. Colt had a better chance at earning a scholarship in wrestling—and already the U.S. Naval Academy as well as some schools here in the Midwest were interested in him.

There were outside factors as well that Mike and Colt had to battle. A few people in town believed that Colt would not have returned punts as a freshman, logged significant playing time last year as a sophomore, or start this year as a junior if Mike were not on the coaching staff. It was nonsense; Colt might not have been the Redmen's best player, but he certainly was among their top three. Still, the displays of jealousy wore on Mike. At wrestling matches, when Colt was on his back after a rare takedown, the crowd would cheer in full-throated lust in the hope that they were about to witness his first defeat.

"It's not a great feeling to have the whole gym rooting against your son," Mike said. "Half the time, my heart breaks for him."

Game time was drawing near, and Mike smiled as he headed for the locker room. "I guess I knew what I was getting into," he said. "It's hard, but I'm glad I'm doing it."

Inside, the Redmen were crammed into this tiny cinder-block box waiting for a pregame talk. Coach Barta did not have a whole lot to say. He believed that his Redmen were several touchdowns better than Plainville, and this was the first and relatively easy step in what he hoped was a long season. Thirty years of coaching had taught him an awful lot about moderation. There was no reason for his team to want to bust out of the locker room chewing glass for a team that was not going to offer much of a challenge.

Coach Barta waded into the middle of the room, his players on their knees surrounding him. He put his hand on a freshman's helmet.

"It starts here, guys," he said in a voice barely above a whisper. "We're going to play hard. We're going to play fast. We're going to play efficient. And, guys, we're going to have?"

He didn't have to let the question hang out there long.

"Fun," the team answered in one voice.

"That's all I got," he said.

The Redmen paired up and clasped hands. They always took the field holding hands, two-by-two and led by the captains. On the far sidelines, where five hundred or so of the Smith Center faithful were seated, a sea of red hats and T-shirts rose to attention. When the Redmen burst through a banner held by the cheerleaders, they roared and horns honked from the cars and trucks circling the field. I looked to midfield, where the Cardinals had stopped their pregame drills to watch the Redmen's entrance. In the Plainville grandstands, the Cardinals' parents also were on their feet, transfixed by the spectacle. Smith Center might as well have been the New York Giants.

"Look up there," said Cole Conaway, an ebullient freshman who liked to chat throughout practice and games.

Overhead in a cloudless blue sky, two dozen turkey buzzards circled from one goalpost to the other.

"They're here for them," said Cole, pointing across the field at the Cardinals, a goofy grin growing beneath his face mask.

The only thing more intimidating than the Redmen's entrance was the team's opening act. On the first play of scrimmage, Colt Rogers took a handoff, scooted behind Justin Nixon's ample rear end, and disappeared for a moment. Suddenly, he bounced out of a pile and galloped down the left sidelines sixty-six yards for a touchdown. The next time the Redmen had the ball it took them only four plays to score, the time after that just six plays, and finally just a single play; this time it was Joe Osburn, who burst fifty-two yards down the right sideline. While the national record the Redmen had set the previous year for most points in a first quarter was not in danger, it was about as good as a start for a season as could have been scripted. In the opening ten minutes of the game, the Redmen were up, 28–0. Halfway through the second quarter, they reached forty points and the "mercy rule" was in effect, and the clock kept running.

It was hard to tell whether Smith Center was that good or Plainville was that bad. The Redmen, as promised, hit hard. Early in the first quarter, Marshall McCall put his helmet on the Plainville quarterback, Ross Copeland, and brought roars of appreciation from the Smith Center sideline. Copeland was slow to get up, while Marshall bounced to his feet.

Two plays later, however, Marshall was the one on his

knees, unsure of where he was. It took the trainer fifteen seconds of hearing Marshall babble to diagnose a concussion.
He was disoriented, and his eyes were glazed. When Coach
Barta told him he was done for the day, Marshall had trouble pulling words from his throat, but still he protested. He
put on his helmet and started back into the huddle.

"I'm good, Coach," Marshall grunted through his mouth-
guard.

Mike Rogers grabbed one arm and Travis Rempe the
other.

"No, Marshall, you might as well go get dressed because
you're done until a doctor says otherwise," Coach Barta
said.

Shane McCall was now standing behind his son. Marshall's mother, Susan, appeared, too. Her lips were trembling
as the trainer told the McCalls that Marshall had suffered a
concussion. (When they returned home, Susan would wake
Marshall every two hours until they got to a doctor in the
morning.) Susan slipped an arm around her son and held
him tight at the waist. His fellow captains came by.

"We're OK here, Marsh," said Trenton Terrill. "We got a
lot of football left to play this season."

Marshall was white, and his eyes glistened. He trembled
slightly and nodded.

When the first half came to an end, the score was 49–0 in
favor of the Redmen. The junior varsity played most of the
second half, and between their inexperience and the running
clock, it was a more competitive game. Sort of. The final
score was Smith Center 63, Plainville 6. The two teams lined
up and shook hands, and then the Redmen amassed near the
end zone and took a knee.

Landon Hubbard, a senior, climbed into the middle of

the pack. He had to quit playing for the Redmen after his sophomore season after a series of stingers exposed a flaw in his spine. He was just one awful hit away from permanent paralysis. Still, Landon rode the bus to games and roamed the sidelines in his game jersey. He also was the son of the pastor of the Evangelical Free Church, and he led the players-only prayer the Redmen said after each game.

Waiting fifteen yards away were the Smith Center cheerleaders and some of the other junior high and high school girls. When the prayer broke up, they sang the song that they have been singing to their boys for decades.

*We love you, Redmen, oh yes we do.*
*We love you, Redmen, oh yes we do.*
*When you're not with us, we're blue.*
*Oh, Redmen, we love you!*

They blew the players kisses and repeated the whole ritual one more time.

Then all the kids joined their parents, who also had flooded the south end of the stadium. Justin Nixon and his brother Josh stood with their father as their mother, Marsha, took photographs. Some of the players made plans to dress fast and get out of town. The Kansas State Fair was under way in Hutchinson, about three hours south of here, and the cows and hogs these boys were showing in competition were already there. Now they would drive through the night in time to present them.

Coach Barta ambled into the middle of the crowd, and a circle began to form around him. After each home game the men in town circled up in the locker room, crossing their arms in front of them to clasp the hands of those next to them. Everyone was welcome: fathers, grandfathers, former players, and fathers of former players. After away games, when the Redmen circled up on the field, women also were a part of the chain. Now, the circle was at least four hundred folks strong, a loving embrace of all things Smith Center.

"Look around you, guys. Do you think you have enough support?" the coach said. "These are the people that make you special and our school special and our town special. I don't have a whole lot to say, except congratulations. Coach Hutch?"

Big Hutch held Brock's hand on one side and Justin's on the other. He shook his head and let a smile grow into a grin. "That was a pretty good first game," he said. "We've got some things to work on, and we will. Good job."

"Coach Rogers," said Coach Barta, who had now been absorbed into the circle.

"I think when people around the state of Kansas pick up the newspaper tomorrow and see the score of this game," Mike said, "they're going to have to think twice about all that talk of Smith Center not being as good as we've been in the past. You've put them on notice."

"Coach Hutch," said Coach Barta.

"Who hits harder?" Brock asked in a low voice.

"We do," answered the Redmen in even tones, so as not to show up the home team.

"I can't wait for practice next week," Brock said. "Way to go."

"Coach Wilson," said Coach Barta.

"That was a good first step on our journey," said Tim Wilson. "Like we talk about, every day we're going to get a little bit better, and our next game will be a better game. Nice job."

"Who's got a little prayer for us?" asked Coach Barta.

"I do, Coach," answered Trenton Terrill.

Everyone in the circle bowed his or her head.

"Lord, thank you for allowing us the opportunity to play this great game of football," Trenton said, "and we are grateful for our friends, family, and community that came out to support us. Let's also pray for our friend Marshall, that he will heal up. Amen."

# 6

I like the competition all right, but I'm really going to miss the guys the most. I get enough competition at the stock shows and fairs, but working a farm can be, well, lonely.

—Cody Tucker, September 12, 2008

Big Hutch walked off the field with a lopsided grin, squinting against the mist blowing in his face.

"We've been in a few of these over the years," he told me. Still, he was strangely energized by what had occurred in the first half of the Redmen's home opener against the Trego Golden Eagles. "We're putting the ball on the ground too much."

The Redmen, indeed, had been unable to hang on to the ball in a warm, persistent rain and had fumbled four times. Twice, the Golden Eagles had recovered it, thwarting two certain Smith Center scores. It was the reason the numbers on the scoreboard looked absolutely shocking: Home 8, Visitor 0. The one scoring drive was bruising, however, consuming a full seven minutes of the second quarter as the Redmen covered seventy-five yards by handing the ball a half-dozen times to fullback Trevor Rempe, who rammed through the middle of the line like a bulldozer.

In the closing minutes of the half, Leo Tuxhorn, the Redmen's usually stoic manager, voiced what most Smith Center fans were thinking. Leo was seventy-eight and had walked these sidelines for twenty-three years. He was a decorated Korean War veteran and for more than thirty years had run the army's National Guard unit here well enough to recruit more than 1,200 young people into military service and earn a spot in the state's National Guard Hall of Fame.

Leo also was fighting a losing battle with the hearing aids he wore in both ears, so when he made a declaration it reverberated up and down the sidelines and into the lower rows of the stands.

"I cannot remember the last time we failed to score in the first quarter," he said.

Coach Barta stood at the door of the locker room as his team filed past at halftime. He waited for Doug Boucher, Darren Sasse, and Nate Smith—another former Redman who was currently student teaching to finish his degree—to come down from the press box. They were perched there every game, charting plays and passing on observations through the wireless headsets the coaches wore on the sidelines.

"You guys seeing anything I'm missing?" he asked.

"We're turning it over and committing too many penalties," said Doug Boucher.

Coach Barta nodded. He, too, seemed unusually delighted by his team's poor play in the first half. He even took responsibility for a pair of fumbles by his quarterbacks. He was still alternating Travis Rempe and Ethan Eastes at the position, which he believed contributed to the botched snaps.

"We have to decide soon on one of them if we're going to develop any rhythm," the coach said. "I want one of them to take the job, and right now they're too comfortable sharing it."

Before kickoff, Coach Barta had leaned against the chainlink fence outside the locker room and watched the Golden Eagles warm up. Trego had only twenty-three kids in pads, a fraction of the number Coach Barta had coached there in the 1970s when he was starting his career as an assistant football coach. This was before the population drain had forced the consolidation of school districts, and the Golden Eagles were WaKeeney's team, the biggest town and county seat of Trego County.

"We'd get eighty or ninety kids out each year and competed for the state title every fall," Coach Barta said. "We were a dynasty, and I thought it would go on forever. I almost didn't take this job. But things disappear a lot quicker than it takes you to build them up."

Coach Barta had built a dynasty here in Smith Center, and the evidence went beyond the Redmen's impressive record. It was behind him in the parking lot of Hubbard Stadium, which was already filled an hour before game time. It was in the long line snaking beyond the outdoor grills—local businesses were on a wait list for the honor of hosting the free tailgate that preceded each home game. It was here along this fence where Dave Mace, John Terrill, and Jay Overmiller watched their sons do the same warm-up drills they had done twenty and thirty years ago when they were Redmen.

"What are you so happy about, Jay?" Coach Barta asked.

"It's football season, Coach," he said. "Ball games are my social hour. I spend enough time alone on the farm. This is where I get to catch up with people and watch my boys."

Coach Barta turned his gaze to his own team, fifty-six

members strong, painstakingly going through their pre-game stretches. He knew he had his work cut out for him this season, and for the first time ever he was thinking seriously about how he would know when he had had enough of coaching.

"You know, life is basically doing the same thing everybody else does every day," he told me before the game. "Fulfilling lives come with doing these things with passion, working constantly on the details that no one but you really sees. It's what we try to pass on to each group of guys we have, that, and the ability to live in harmony with others. It's not just the foundation of our football program, either. Hopefully, in ten or fifteen years, when it matters, these guys will think about something they learned here and make the right decision and have a little success."

He left unsaid whether his own passion was still engaged by doing the same thing day after day. Coach Barta still had plenty to pass on to young men, but perhaps more than that, he believed that he still had much to learn from them. He was a self-described borrower, taking positive thinking and visualization tenets from New Age spiritualists as well as organizational principles from business and leadership books. When U.S. Army recruiters came to Smith Center High School, Coach Barta asked them to address the team and take questions about how they came to the military and their life within it. He did the same with former players and visiting coaches, even reporters and sportswriters who took advantage of the Redmen's open-door policy. He wanted to expose his boys to as many different viewpoints and life experiences as he could. He remained curious about life beyond his town as well.

Coach Barta worked hard not only to honor the bonds

between fathers and sons and the community of men, but also to show by example that they could express how they felt about one another. That's what the postgame circle-ups were all about: being grateful, honest, and loving to one another.

Like virtually everyone in this part of western Kansas, Coach Barta believed personal faith was important, but that it also was a private matter. He was Roman Catholic, but he understood that there were ten other churches in town and that prayer was part of the community fabric. He incorporated that as well into his football program.

Now, with the score 8–0 at halftime, there was no doubt that Coach Barta was engaged as he walked into the locker room. The Redmen were crowded around the blackboard, waiting. Trevor and Travis Rempe sat in the front, looking more puzzled than panicked. Colt Rogers's jaw was slack. Justin Nixon had his eyes closed. Even as immature as this group was, they understood that they had moved the ball at will, gaining more than 270 yards, and should have been up by three or four touchdowns.

Coach Barta picked up a piece of chalk and scrawled "8–0" on the blackboard. Then he circled it. Once, twice, three times.

"We haven't been in a game like this in how many years?" he asked as he turned around. He searched the locker room, hitching up his khaki pants, hoping for an answer.

"It's kind of fun, isn't it, guys?" he asked.

The players apparently didn't share their coach's sense of joy in being in a close contest. They remained stone-faced.

Coach Barta smiled broadly.

"I'm going to let the coaches talk to you about specific adjustments," he told them. "I think you're wearing them down, and all I want is for you guys to go out and have fun this next half."

Big Hutch paced back and forth, the half smile still on his face as Tim Wilson spoke to the linemen. Tim had red hair, a schoolboy's face, and the soul of a farmer. He helped his dad mostly, but also had two hundred acres of his own that he worked for a few extra dollars and to stay rooted and relaxed. He had Coach Barta's implacable nature and the patience of a special education teacher, which he had been for the bulk of his teaching career. He was crouched in a wide stance before Justin and the other linemen.

"Get your head across them now," he said. "When we do that, we can move them into the parking lot."

Mike Rogers was even briefer. "We got to take care of the ball," he said, staring at Colt, who had lost a fumble in the first half.

Little Hutch frantically drew a series of adjustments on the chalkboard that looked like hieroglyphics and sounded like a weather report. "Let's show them more Miami storm, and more lightning," he said, referring to various alignments.

Coach Barta stayed on the edge of the room. When his team started pairing up and clasping hands to take the field for the second half, he stopped them in front of the door. "Longer you let them play with you," he warned, "the more confidence they're going to gain. Let's make them quit."

Marshall McCall led the Redmen onto the field. He wore his no. 29 jersey but with jeans and without shoulder pads since he was still recovering from the concussion he had suffered the previous week. So far, his senior season had consisted of one tremendous hit and three wobbly offensive plays. Marshall was bummed and more than a little spooked. He had little memory of the Plainville game. His headaches had come and gone all week. Worse, Marshall felt like a lousy captain standing on the side of the practice field the past four days. To stay engaged in the Trego game, he grabbed a towel and planted himself on the yard marker next to the linesman. He wiped dry each football and made sure dry ones were in play. This had not been the role he had hoped to play in his senior season.

When the Redmen went sixty-four yards for a touchdown on their first possession of the second half, the crowd at Hubbard field relaxed and anticipated the coming rout now that the score was 14–0. But on their next series, Colt let the ball squirt from his hands. He was able to get it back, but on the sidelines Mike Rogers grimaced. He started to say something but thought better of it. The very next play, however, Travis Rempe botched a handoff, and this time the Golden Eagles recovered.

Marshall left his spot by the linesman and went first to Travis, who was squatting on the sidelines holding his head in his hands and cussing himself. Travis's inability to control his emotions had worried the coaches and had kept him from winning the quarterback job outright.

"Let it go, Travis," Marshall told him, slapping him on the shoulder pads. "We need you clear-headed."

With Colt, Marshall merely offered a quick slap on the bottom. He knew nobody was as hard on Colt as Colt was on himself.

But the Smith Center defense held, and soon the Barta-Bone was in full, devastating motion. Joe Osburn burst over right tackle for touchdown runs of twenty-seven and thirty-three yards. Colt blasted over the left side and got loose for a seventy-six-yard touchdown. Suddenly, the score was 34–0, and junior varsity players were running on and off the field.

The rain had stopped, and the autumn air felt like air-conditioning. Next to me, I heard someone say, "I'm really going to miss this next year."

It was Cody Tucker, the senior right offensive tackle. He was listed on the program at 220 pounds, but as I learned throughout the season, kids in western Kansas were rarely as big as they were on the roster sheet. Cody was square-jawed, with a full head of blond hair. He favored cowboy boots and a ball cap with a bowed bill advertising the business that he and his younger brother Van had started; CV GELBVIEH, PORTIS KANSAS was stitched front and center. The CV was for Cody and Van, and Gelbvieh is a prized breed of cattle that they bought and sold and showed at livestock shows across the country. In effect, as the brothers explained to me, they would buy a Gelbvieh as a yearling for anywhere from eight hundred to two thousand dollars—though they could cost a great deal more—and then serve as its personal trainer. They fed, fattened, and got it fit and pretty to compete in competitions for prize money. They were good at it, recently winning their class at the Kansas State Fair, and finishing in the money at prestigious events such as the National Western Livestock Show held each January in Denver. When the Tuckers' cows were finished with their competitive careers, they ended up where their brethren usually did: on someone's plate.

The Tuckers and the other farm kids on the Redmen were among the most relaxed and genial members of the team. They were literally grounded in the earth and spent virtually all of their waking hours working because the chores on a farm are never-ending. Their labor started at six in the morning and ended at nine thirty at night. They lived on a farm seventeen miles south of town and mostly saw their friends at school. Football was truly a game to them, a few hours a day to spend with their buddies rather than family farmhands or junior livestock moguls.

"I like the competition all right, but I'm really going to miss the guys the most," Cody continued. "I get enough competition at the stock shows and fairs, but working a farm can be, well, lonely."

A few moments later, with the junior varsity on the field, the number "56" rose above the visitors' grandstands and lit up the sky. No one had warned me about the winning streak clock, which first appeared the previous season. It was the idea of Gayle and Kristi Jones, the owners of Jones Machinery, who fashioned it from a forklift and Christmas lights. They raised it in their parking lot, and it lit up a sliver of wheat field and silhouetted the old tractors that lay idle outside their workshop. It was my first inkling of how much the town wanted its place in the high school record books.

The final seconds were ticking off the clock as Trego was being sent home in defeat, 42–8. The Redmen crossed the field to shake the hands of the Golden Eagles. As soon as the handshakes were finished, Coach Barta and his assistants and his headset guys met at midfield. The coach was superstitious; before they went onto the field with the team, they all shook hands and wished each other luck. After each game, they met again and offered congratulatory handshakes. Their postgame mood tonight was hardly grave, but it was not celebratory either. The Redmen had fumbled six times and had committed six penalties for sixty-five yards. One of the penalties had nullified a touchdown. The coaching staff still had plenty of work to do.

It was men-only back in the locker room for the circle-up, and as Coach Barta drifted to the middle, he recognized a mood from his players that he did not like.

"You're 2–0 so don't hang your heads," he said.

The players looked up and reached for the hands of their fathers and their teammates' fathers.

"I liked your effort out there tonight, guys," the coach said. "Remember we're a work in progress."

For thirty years now, Friday nights were a reason to celebrate in Smith Center, and as Hubbard Stadium emptied, a variety of postgame parties filled up. They were called "Fifth Quarters," and they broke out at Pooches and at Duffy's, a steakhouse, as well as in private homes throughout town. The churches took turns holding Fifth Quarters for the junior high school kids, giving them somewhere to dance and play games and allowing their parents an opportunity to go out, too.

Mary and I were invited to the home of Steve and Janet Kloster, who were having a small crowd over for steak soup. Steve had attended Cleveland Chiropractic College in Kansas City, my hometown, and the Klosters had a nephew attending my old high school. They had discovered Smith Center after he had graduated and was looking to buy an already established practice. They had raised their three children here, and even though their youngest, a daughter, was already a senior at Kansas State, they were still involved with Smith Center High School.

Steve and Janet were among the many folks who supported the high school behind the scenes. They wrote checks and bought raffle tickets, and Steve worked on the school's athletes for free. He had also become enamored of wrestling and often drove hours to watch the Redmen's meets. The previous year at the state championship tournament, Steve had come out of the stands and worked on the boys between matches. Like everyone else in town, Steve and Janet thought whatever they did for the high school was not enough—let alone anything to be recognized for.

"Everyone wants his or her kids to have some success," Steve told us. "Here that desire spills over to all kids, probably because we watch them all grow up."

As gratified and as proud as Steve was of the football team's winning streak, he had a theory that the town would show its best self when it was finally snapped. "No one will be sad or shocked," he said. "I believe we'll take care of the players on the team. We'll let them know they mean more than winning football games."

———

Coach Barta handed Big Hutch a glass of strawberry soda and a scouting report. Mike, Tim, and Little Hutch were in front of their lockers and changing into their coaching shorts.

"This may be the week," Coach Barta said.

Everyone knew what he was talking about.

"We're really not very good," said Big Hutch.

"They got some players," offered Mike.

The staff had spent the previous Sunday afternoon over in the NASA Lab, breaking down the game film of next week's opponent, the Norton Bluejays. They spent most of their fall weekends in that darkened room, preparing what had become known as epic scouting reports. Tim and Little Hutch did the heavy lifting—charting each offensive and defensive play, what alignment the opponent was in, as well as what down and how much yardage were needed for a first down. The images on the screen whirred forward and backward, as Big Hutch and Mike Rogers offered running commentary, often from the floor where they were stretched out and had their heads on pillows.

Coach Barta mostly listened and watched intently as if it were the first time he had seen a high school game. Now, after digesting what he had seen from the Bluejays, he and his coaches knew they had a very good chance of losing on Friday night.

Norton was one of Smith Center's oldest rivals. The Bluejays had more kids in school than the Redmen and played in Class 3A. On Friday, they would have bigger kids on the field, too, especially their star running back, a six-foot, 210-pound sophomore named Terrell Lane. He was both the rare African American and the rare big-time college prospect in western Kansas. He was fast and powerful. Beyond his talent, his reputation had grown to mythical proportions because he was supposedly the cousin or half-brother or nephew (no one was sure which) of Cedric Benson, then a running back for the Chicago Bears. It also was an away game, and the Redmen did not usually play well in Norton, which was sixty miles due west of town on Highway 36. Two years before, Smith Center had barely escaped with a 14–3 victory, and in 2003 the Bluejays had won on their home field, 17–8. It was the last time the Redmen had lost a regular-season game.

"We're twenty points better than them," said Brock Hutchinson, chasing the negative thoughts from the room.

Brock had been a defensive back at Fort Hays State and had a head for solving the problems presented by the other team's offense. At thirty-four, he was the youngest member of the staff and had maintained the shape of an athlete, thin and sinewy. He stalked the practice field like a prairie bob-cat, beating the players to spots on the field and herding them from drill to drill. With his close-cropped hair and un-lined face, Brock looked like just another high school senior on the sidelines rather than the father of four that he was. He was also as competitive as his players. As the varsity wrestling coach, he had led Smith Center to state champion-ships in the previous two years. He did so by getting on the mat with each wrestler, regardless of weight class, and ab-sorbing as well as dishing out beatings. Brock also admitted what the players were banned from doing, and the other coaches didn't dare say: that keeping the winning streak in-tact meant a hell of a lot to him.

"Yeah, I feel the pressure every day, every week," he had told me as we rode the bus to Plainville. "Last year, it didn't mean anything, partly because we were basically unbeat-able. I mean, we had forty points and the clock running every game before halftime. We would be home by 9:00 p.m. But last year, the streak was just a number; we were still a season away from achieving it.

"It's right in our grasp," he continued. "If we win thir-teen games and the championship, we will have the longest winning streak in the history of Kansas high school football. I want that. These guys want it. The whole town wants it."

Now, Brock grabbed a stack of scouting reports, walked into the locker room, and began handing them out to his players. For Norton, the report ran thirty pages, and Brock was proud of it. He should have been; it was as comprehen-sive and clearly presented as the scouting reports I had seen at collegiate powerhouses like Florida State. The players' fathers could hardly wait until their boys got home to see what Brock and Tim had compiled. By Wednesday, the guys at the Second Cup Café and folks throughout town would be talking about its contents and would have a good idea of what to expect from the Bluejays.

Before they read, watched, and listened to Brock and Tim tell them every tendency and weakness Norton had, and how they were going to exploit it, Coach Barta recited the keys to the game, which he had written on the cover of the scouting report.

1. We must improve this week and start executing consistently.
2. They are a big play team, we must run the ball and hit.
3. Special teams will be very important—must execute.
4. They have some very good players. Best runner #1 and #33. Favorite receiver #6, #1, #88.
5. This will be #1 week.

Then he quit reading and said: "You all know about Lane. He's a very good running back, probably one of the best you're going to see. We must know where he is, and wear him out by hitting him every play. It should be a great game."

# 7

I want all you guys to know that I love each and every one of you, and my heart would break if anything happened to one of you."
—Roger Barta, September 16, 2008

The Redmen were not focused in practice the following afternoon, and Coach Barta was frustrated. After thirty years, he knew each team was different, and every one of them had needed "their minds worked a little bit." He had entered the season expecting that this bunch was going to get psychic overhaul. Still, they were testing his patience. Just because Coach Barta was not a screamer, it did not mean he did not have a temper. Like a volcano, he erupted rarely, and stories about former players getting him to that point were legend and the best deterrent to players breaking his rules.

His son, Brooks, was a fullback and linebacker on the 1986 state championship team when he committed a mortal sin against Redmen football. One game, he forgot his helmet.

The rule was straightforward: no helmet, no playing time. Brooks told Big Hutch about his dilemma, and his father's number-one assistant came up with a novel solution. He found a freshman who was willing to "rent" his helmet to

Brooks for ten dollars. Neither Brooks nor Big Hutch, however, was prepared for the guilt they felt as Coach Barta blistered the freshman for the transgression.

"Brooks had his head down," Big Hutch said. "I had my head down. We were afraid to tell him until ten years later."

About halfway through practice, Marshall McCall brought Coach Barta's temper to full boil. It was his first practice in pads since his concussion, and the coach had insisted that he wear a revolution helmet, which had been designed with extra padding for maximum protection from head injuries. Marshall was having a hard time adjusting to the extra weight, and some teammates who thought the helmet looked funny were razzing him. Colt Rogers, especially, was on Marshall's case. Even though half the Redmen already wore the newfangled helmet, Colt and Marshall had challenged each other to be tougher, more old-school. So Marshall sent Brody Frieling, one of the water boys, up to the locker room for his old helmet. He thought no one would notice.

Coach Barta did. In fact, he had overheard Colt and the other players teasing Marshall. When Marshall lined up behind the quarterback, the coach told him to sit down.

"You're through," he said.

Marshall mumbled something about how he was more comfortable in his old helmet.

"Do you want to play on this team?" Coach Barta asked. "If you do, you better do as you're told."

Marshall spent the rest of the practice on the sideline. When practice was over, and the team was gathering for final remarks, the coach was still upset. He didn't raise his voice, but he got after Marshall again for thinking he knew better than the coach. By the time he dismissed the team, there was not a single Redman who did not feel sorry for their teammate. It was the quietest locker room of the season as they showered quickly and escaped immediately.

They were still chastened when Coach Barta walked to the middle of the locker room the next afternoon. He stood there until he was certain that he had everyone's attention. The coach had spoken to Marshall earlier in the day. He thought he had been too rough on him, and it had kept him up the previous night.

"I got on Marshall pretty good last night," Coach Barta said. "He came to me today and we talked. We understand each other. Since I got on him in front of you, I wanted to apologize to him in front of everybody. I want all you guys to know that I love each and every one of you, and my heart would break if anything happened to one of you.

"I don't know the science behind helmets and concussions," he continued. "I do know that these new helmets cost $187 versus $117 for the older ones. I'm responsible for you guys out here. I want you safe. So let's not mess around."

Coach Barta then walked to the west wall, where Marshall sat with the other seniors.

"I'm sorry," he said, and offered his hand.

He was not finished, however, and a sense of gloom hovered in the locker room. Coach Barta returned to the middle of the room.

"There's something else we need to talk about," he said. "First I want everyone on the floor doing push-ups while I talk."

The freshmen hit the floor immediately. The seniors glanced furtively at one another and took the floor, and soon it was a sea of white shirts moving up and down. Coach Barta stood in their midst.

"I told you I was upset last night, and I stayed here to think about things," he said. "Well, when I was finally ready to leave, I stopped by the bathroom stall over there and it was filled with . . . well . . . all I can say is—it was a master-piece."

Snickers wafted up from the floor, and Coach Barta turned up the volume on a growl. "Man, I would have been proud of it, too."

The sea of push-ups became a storm of laughter.

"It couldn't have been a freshman that did that—they are way too little," he continued.

The Redmen collapsed on the floor and were laughing.

"I've been retired now a few years, and I don't know what they're teaching over there in health class," he said. "But let me enlighten you about toilets—you see, there's a lever up there. And, if you pull it, whatever is in there disap-pears. It's like magic."

Coach Barta let his players howl for a little longer.

"Coach Hutch," he said.

It was time to get back to business. The players were on their feet and putting their helmets on. Big Hutch rose, too.

"Let's go flush Norton, boys," he roared.

Everyone headed for the doors with smiles. Lightness had returned to Redmen world.

———

It was the night before the Norton game, and the Redmen were piling into Marshall's clubhouse, getting ready to settle in for some pregame camaraderie. Not everyone was here; the "country boys," as the Tuckers and the other Future Farmers of America were known, were no-shows. Marshall had a movie ready to put in, and some of the seniors draped themselves over the club chairs. Justin and Josh Nixon drifted at the edge of the room with their hands jammed in their pockets, looking at the posters they had seen a million times. Dillon Corbett and Logan Tuxhorn, both juniors, sat by themselves in a corner.

Kris Lehmann and Joe Osburn volleyed the Ping-Pong ball back and forth. They had become close over the summer and were thinking of getting tattoos together after the season was over. Kris was not only the reason Joe came out for football, but also why Joe was still toeing Coach Barta's line.

At first glance, they were a mismatched duo. Kris was a six-footer, 210 pounds, and carved perfectly from what looked like stone. He had been a starter as a junior and was a captain now. He also was an honors student with a 1950s brush cut that made him look like he was from the era of Johnny Unitas. He looked you in the eye, dotted his conversation with *sirs* and *ma'ams*, and moved easily among the various subsets of the team.

Joe was moody and a subset all his own. He rarely spoke and held himself apart from the crowd. It was a quality that both touched and frustrated the coaches. The previous season, after the Redmen had won their sixth straight game and were officially crowned the Mid-Continent League champions, Brock Hutchinson found Joe on the sideline crying. He thought that Joe might have injured himself somehow.

"Coach, I've never won any kind of championship before," he told Brock.

Joe's pain was rooted in his biological family. His mother and father drank. He and his brother Jon had come to Robert and Kim Osburn as foster kids when they were eleven and ten years old. They were old enough then to understand that they had been neglected. Joe remained young enough now to think that it was his fault he was separated from his parents, and he believed he could somehow make it all better the next time. A couple of years ago, he had run away to Kansas City to find them. The visit had not gone well.

Joe told Kris that he intended to find his parents again. He would be eighteen in December, which would legally make him an adult. He also would be off probation for a break-in that he had been a part of in Weskan. Joe had been drinking when it occurred, but he had stayed out of trouble since.

Kris was not sure if Joe was serious about running away, but he was certain it would not happen during the football season. Joe was just learning how talented he was, and he enjoyed the attention he received.

There was no mistaking the tension that coursed through Marshall's clubhouse. It had little to do with pregame jitters and everything to do with not yet knowing and trusting one another. The players acted as if they were supposed to be here rather than wanted to be here. What had been so organic and natural for the previous year's senior class—embracing one another—had not yet taken hold of this bunch of Redmen.

Suddenly, there was pounding on the walls, followed by the giggles of high school girls. The players were startled at first but then gave chase. As they piled out the door, they looked relieved to be free of one another.

———

As the Smith Center bus rolled into Norton on Friday afternoon, there was little doubt that this was the biggest game in northwest Kansas this weekend. Signs were hung throughout town, threatening the Redmen with a certain loss. Little kids gave the bus the thumbs-down sign as they walked home from school. And, with the game still nearly three hours away, folks were already showing up at the stadium, which was about as Norman Rockwell as small-town sporting venues get.

The football field was down the road from Norton High School and at the bottom of a bowl dug into a hillside. It was adjacent to an automobile racetrack with a perfectly manicured baseball diamond in its infield. Norton's grain elevator watched over the complex, and the sound of train whistles and the rattle of boxcars were part of the warm September night's sound track.

The Redmen had stopped at the high school to put on their pads and uniforms. Coach Barta had warned them against getting distracted by the girls' volleyball practice, which always seemed to be in session whenever Smith Center came west to play the Bluejays.

"We don't want blood flowing where we don't want it to go," he said. "So let's stay focused, and keep your mind on the game."

The Redmen were already on the field when the Bluejays engaged in another piece of gamesmanship. It began with the sound of cleats stomping gravel in the unseen distance. Everyone was looking to the hills, but there was no sign of the invading army. Suddenly, a blue-and-yellow flag was visible on the tree line above the stadium. Then, beneath it, was the entire Norton team, helmets on and holding hands in tight formation. They descended a gravel pathway on the hill, and the stomping became fiercer as they approached the field. They marched past the Redmen to midfield, where they huddled for a long couple of minutes.

"*BLUEJAYS!*" they finally shouted in unison.

It was the kind of high theater that brings goose bumps to all but the most hard-hearted. It also worked at unnerving the Redmen. Marshall McCall, Colt Rogers, and even the normally implacable Justin Nixon looked as if toothpicks had suddenly bridged the space between their cheeks and eyebrows. The whole team was jittery during the pregame as they stole glances at the legend-in-the-making Terrell Lane, who looked even more formidable in person and in pads.

Colt watched Lane cut through an imaginary defense and grimaced. "He looks like an NFL linebacker," he said.

Marshall watched the other Bluejays. "They are big all around," he observed. "It doesn't matter. I'm ten feet off the ground right now. We need to get this thing started."

Coach Barta, too, had big-game adrenaline stirring in him. Instead of letting Brock have the final word of pregame, as was usually the case, Coach Barta stepped forward with a final thought. He held both hands above his head and made sure everyone was listening.

"Guys, I didn't know it was Flag Day," he growled. "We didn't bring one. So let's go get theirs."

He punched the air with an uppercut that brought his team howling and to their feet.

In the game's opening minutes, it looked as if the Redmen might have been overworried about the Bluejays. Joe Osburn got loose for twelve yards, Trevor Rempe banged up the middle for thirteen yards, and in just three plays the Redmen were on Norton's 33-yard line. Then everything went wrong.

First, Smith Center was flagged for a motion penalty, and then Trenton Terrill, the senior center and captain, crumpled, holding his knee. He had to be carried off the field.

The Redmen's drive stalled, and now the mighty Terrell Lane was on the field to face the Smith Center defense for the first time. On Lane's very first carry, Marshall drilled him chest-high and then ran right through him. Lane got up slowly. Marshall leaped to his feet, relieved that his first postconcussion hit had not left him foggy.

When the Bluejays failed to move the ball, Lane dropped back and boomed a punt that Joe Osburn caught and then handed off to Colt. Colt zigged and zagged through defenders and emerged forty-six yards later on Norton's 10-yard line. Behind him, however, was another yellow flag—blocking in the back—and the ball was returned to the Smith Center 44-yard line. Three plays later, Marshall bobbled a handoff from Travis, and the Bluejays had the ball on the Redmen's 40-yard line. When Cody Tucker didn't get on the field on time for a fourth down and one, the Redmen turned the ball over on downs.

"That's on you, Cody," barked Big Hutch as Cody returned to the sideline. "Keep your head in the game."

In the second quarter, it was Colt who made a crucial mistake that led to the first score of the game. The Redmen were backed up to their end zone when Travis handed the ball to Colt. Colt ducked an arm tackle and shot a stiff arm out in search of extra yards. Instead, the ball squirted loose, and the Bluejays recovered on Smith Center's 5-yard line. Mike Rogers hung his head, peeking out of the corner of his eye as his son stalked off the field. On the very next play, Lane blasted into the end zone as the blue-and-yellow-clad fans on Norton's side of the hill went wild. The Bluejays had done something to the Redmen that hadn't happened in years. They took a 7–0 lead.

Coach Barta met his team out on the field.

"Now you're all right," he said. "Let's breathe deep and put a long drive together and get on the board."

Colt returned the kickoff to the 25-yard line, and over the next nine plays the Redmen quieted the celebration on the Norton sidelines. Justin smothered the left side of the line and opened gaping holes for Colt. Trevor Rempe took one hand-off after another from his brother and bludgeoned the middle of the Norton defense. When Trevor, barely 170 pounds, knocked the anvil-sized Lane backward on a seventeen-yard touchdown run, the Smith Center sideline looked like a human popcorn popper.

On defense, Marshall and a pair of juniors, defensive end Jesse Roush and middle linebacker Logan Tuxhorn, were pounding on Lane every play, and Norton had so far failed to make a first down. They pushed the Bluejays back to their own 10-yard line, and Lane was forced to punt once again. This time he shanked it off the side of his foot, and the Redmen got the ball on Norton's 24-yard line. Colt took the ball from Travis, followed Justin, and then cut outside for a touchdown. When Joe Osburn completed the two-point attempt on a quick pitch, the Redmen had a 14–7 lead to take into halftime.

Halftime went by in a blur. The Redmen were beat up and breathing hard. Coach Barta was brief and to the point.

"We have two fumbles and three penalties," he said. "We're killing ourselves. Hold on to the damn ball, and we'll be OK."

Norton, however, was emboldened by the slim margin on the scoreboard. The Redmen managed only one first down for the opening ten minutes of the second half, and on the sidelines the team was getting rattled. Justin was on the freshmen for not having towels and water bottles at the ready as they were supposed to.

"Box it up," he bellowed, and the whole team stepped back two yards off the sidelines to give the coaches more room.

When Terrell Lane broke free of Kris Lehmann at the line of scrimmage and jetted fifty-one yards for a game-tying touchdown, the Redmen were at once panicked and helpless. Marshall felt the game slipping away, and he knew why. The Redmen did not trust one another.

Justin and Trevor, the defensive tackles, were supposed to tie up Norton's interior linemen while the ends, Dillon Corbett and Jesse Roush, were to force the play inside to give the linebackers a clear gap to make the stop. Instead, they all were chasing the ball, trying to make big plays for themselves. Worse was the fact that even as Marshall saw this unfold before him, he could not summon the right words to rally the Redmen. No one could. The huddles were absolutely silent.

Colt and Joe Osburn mishandled the kickoff, and the Redmen found themselves pinned on their own 5-yard line. Colt made up for it, however, when he brushed past Justin's left side and cut behind Kris Lehmann's block and to the sideline. Colt's short legs were pumping up and down like an overworked piston and looked as if they would give out at any second. Instead, he ducked and stumbled and stiff-armed his way the length of the field before a Bluejay caught his toe and he came to a skid at the 1-yard line.

When Trevor ran with the face into the end zone on the following play, and then Joe Osburn skittered in for the two-point conversion, the mood on the Smith Center sideline lifted only a little. There was still a quarter to play, and the Redmen were clinging to a 22–14 lead. But instead of closing the Bluejays out, Smith Center let them back in with another fumble at their own 45-yard line.

On the Norton side of the hill, the crowd was on its feet as the Bluejays handed the ball off to Lane once, twice, three, and four times. It took them eight plays, but now the Bluejays were on the Redmen's 4-yard line, facing fourth down. Marshall, Kris, and Trevor looked at one another. Everyone was breathing hard in the huddle, but none of the captains could think of anything to say.

Lane had taken a beating from the Redmen defense, and blood was oozing from his forearm, where he had had seventeen stitches sewn in at halftime. He already had rumbled for ninety-three yards and had scored two touchdowns; everyone in western Kansas knew who was getting the ball. It didn't matter. The Redmen could not keep Lane out of the end zone. With 6:18 left, Norton had little choice but to go for the two-point conversion and a 22–22 tie.

Brock Hutchinson was on the sideline with his legs spread and his hands on his knees. He dropped his head as soon as Lane got through the Smith Center line. Brock stayed frozen there for a moment. Then he walked out to the field to talk to his defense.

"I don't know what they're talking about over there," he said, jerking his head toward the Norton sideline and knocking his headset askew. "The whole world knows they're going to run the same play, and they're going to run it at you, Kris. Now, let's stop him."

Brock returned to the sideline and reassumed his wide stance. Marshall and Colt inched up to the line from their safety positions and stole glances at each other. Marshall could see in Colt's wide eyes something he rarely saw: fear.

Brock was correct. Lane ran to the left, but Trevor and Dillon and Justin had tied up the line of scrimmage, and the running back could not get his legs churning. Kris, Marshall, Colt, and a swarm of white jerseys buried Lane a yard short of the goal line. As they untangled themselves from the pile, they looked relieved rather than triumphant. The score was 22–20, with six long minutes left to play.

"You had to have that stop," Coach Barta said, meeting his team out on the field. "Let's hold that ball with both hands, open up some holes, run the clock, and get out of town."

They did, barely. Marshall sealed the victory with an interception on the final play. He had caused a fumble earlier and hounded Lane throughout the game. He had played well, but the Redmen had not. Their performance made him sick to his stomach.

"That was a fun game," said Coach Barta as the Smith Center faithful circled up.

"It was a fun game to watch, and you won because you competed, and that's what you need to learn to do. We've got to get a little bit better. You hurt yourself a bunch, but we'll work on that."

Coach Barta knew that his team had been lucky to survive three fumbles and ten penalties that had cost the Redmen seventy precious yards. This should have been the week that the winning streak was snapped at fifty-six games. Instead, the streak was alive at fifty-seven.

"We need to keep Trenton in our prayers," he said. "Hopefully he just has a sprain. I know God doesn't care about wins and losses, but he cares about how we are and how we lead our lives."

# 8

I'm sure he knows how hard I work, and I hope he
understands that I want him to be as proud of me as
I am of him.
                              —Colt Rogers, September 24, 2008

It was Nerd Day at Smith Center High, and Colt Rogers
wore thick-framed glasses, a lopsided red bow tie over an
unevenly buttoned blue shirt, and twisted suspenders. He
sported what we used to call flood pants, which hovered
high above his white socks. It was homecoming week, and
each day featured a theme at school such as Twins Day or
Spirit Day. On Saturday—the morning after the Redmen's
game against Phillipsburg—a parade would kick off Old
Settlers Day, which focused the whole town on its 137-year
history not only as a place of commerce but also as home to
six generations of Kansans.

It was a big week, and Colt was beginning it as sore as he
had ever been. He couldn't make it out of bed to hunt the
morning after the Norton game. He was not the only bat-
tered Redman. Justin Nixon roamed Myers Hardware stiff-
legged the day after the game. The Rempe twins were at
Sunday Mass sitting completely upright, and it was because
of their stiff necks rather than their sense of piety. And Tren-

ton Terrill was in a knee brace with a torn ligament, out for at least eight weeks and perhaps the entire season.

In his nerd get-up, Colt hardly looked seventeen years old, or the preternaturally gifted youngster who as a twelve-year-old, family lore goes, bagged a pair of deer that had wandered within twenty feet of him moments after his dad told him to shoot anything that moved. He did not even look like a sullen teenager feuding with his parents.

Instead, he looked boyish, tentative, like an elementary school student who had snuck into the high school and might be found out at any moment.

The hallways were bustling all around him with kids in garish costumes that would not be out of place backstage at the circus. Marshall McCall rushed by, sporting a rainbow wig and wearing a wrestling singlet. Matt Atwood, a junior defensive end with a cast on his foot, apparently had not bought into the Redmen's vow to swear off girls. He was holding hands with his girlfriend, Whitney, and the couple was oblivious to a gaggle of girls in pigtails, knee socks, and dyed dresses who nearly knocked them over.

Greg Koelsch stood in the hallway and watched the high-spirited parade pass. There was no mistaking him for anyone other than Smith Center High School's principal; he was the only adult male in the building who wore a tie.

"Hey, Mr. Koelsch," said Taylor Arnold, one of the Lady Red's top volleyball players and the girl Trevor Rempe had stopped dating due to football season.

"Taylor," he said with a nod and a smile.

Because he was the principal, Greg had to be both more formal and more reserved than the rest of the faculty. Greg Hobelmann, the athletic director, lived in red-and-white Smith Center polo shirts and windbreakers and could not make it through the hallways without slapping five and patting shoulders. Julie Hutchinson, Brock's wife and a special education teacher, usually had kids hugging her from both sides. The faculty's commitment to the community was all-encompassing. Every teacher in the district was front and center before the town and its children for at least fourteen hours a day.

They coached, ran dance teams and concession stands, mounted plays and vocal competitions, and oversaw the production of yearbooks, art, and service projects. It was the reason Smith Center High School excelled far beyond sports.

With a budget of five million dollars annually, the district was able to pay teachers an average salary of forty thousand dollars. It augmented that base pay with an aggressive incentive structure that tied teachers' extracurricular duties to their salaries. There was a scale of anywhere from 2 to 16 percent to compensate the staff for the time they spent in after-school activities. The bonus for being a head coach, for example, was 12 percent above a teacher's salary. That meant as their teaching salaries increased, so did their coaching salaries. It was one of the reasons the school district was able to retain committed teachers. The other was that the profession here was regarded as noble and worth pursuing.

Greg Koelsch was in his fourth year as principal, and he felt fortunate for a lot of reasons. Not the least of them was that he had yet to expel anyone from the high school. The students here were by no means angels; he had handed out suspensions for cutting class and fighting and rude behavior. Three times a year, however, he brought in a drug dog and had yet to find marijuana, crystal meth, cocaine, or worse. Instead, about as bad as it got were shotgun shells left over from early morning hunting excursions. What he appreciated the most, however, was the parents' willingness to tackle problems head-on. They were vigilant.

Earlier this week, for example, Greg had asked students to supply the names of any homecoming dates who did not go to Smith Center High School. On Nerd Day, he had spent the morning on the phone with the principals of those neighboring high schools trying to find out what kind of kids these were. So far, they had all checked out, but if he had been told that a young man or young woman was a potential problem, he would not allow the teenager to attend the Smith Center homecoming dance.

"I know our parents would back me up," he said.

After school that day, Colt gave me a ride to the football complex. He was smart, an honors student who carried a 3.8 average and wanted to become an architect. The U.S. Naval Academy was interested in having Colt on its wrestling team and had recently sent him a routine questionnaire to fill out. But one of the questions had prompted some soul searching: what is your height and weight?

It was a tormenting reminder of what Colt was afraid was a limitation put on him, over which he had absolutely no control. When he was a boy, his parents had him undergo a variety of tests to see if anything other than genes was responsible for his small stature. There wasn't.

Nobody knew better than Colt that he was small. Still, he did not like talking about his size and instead put in the extra hours in the weight and wrestling and film rooms. He wanted to make certain that his physical stature would never diminish him in athletics.

"How big do you think I am?" he asked me.

He was at once defiant, sad, and convinced that because he was five foot three he was going to be overlooked. Colt was always trying to play bigger and had succeeded in spectacular fashion. He was the Redmen's leading rusher with 558 yards, with a phenomenal average of 14 yards a carry, and had already scored six touchdowns. He was a devastating blocker as well, often flattening linebackers who weighed one hundred pounds more than him. On defense, he played safety and locked down on opposing running backs with perfect tackling form.

The truth was that he was right: if Colt were eight inches taller and seventy pounds heavier, big-time college football coaches would be camped in Smith Center, Kansas.

The role that he couldn't shake, however, was as the Redmen player that opposing teams loved to hate. He had a small man's swagger on the field but hit like a giant. Players jawed at him throughout games. In the stands, parents groused about him. On the high school football Internet message boards, anonymous posters jumped on his mistakes. What fueled the jealousy and resentment was the fact that Colt's father had been one of the greatest Redmen in school history, and he was now his coach.

What they didn't know was how much Colt had already overcome. He was allergic to a lot of foods, as well as to farm life, and twice a week endured three shots of medicine to counteract his allergies. They didn't stop him from eating what he wanted or from working on his grandfather's farm during summers and harvests. Neither did the ring of tissue in his esophagus that had recently been causing him to choke on his food. In a couple of days, the doctors were going to drop a balloon down his throat, blow it up, and tear the ring of tissue apart. Maybe it would keep his esophagus open for a month, maybe forever. Colt never complained about any of these maladies.

He was a tough kid. He knew that people wanted to see him fumble on the football field or get pinned on the wrestling mat. He was self-aware enough to know that he and his father were walking a difficult tightrope as coach and player, as well as father and son. They had been walking it a long time.

"He and my mom have driven me all over the country for wrestling and football since I was five," he said.

It was his father's success in football, however, that Colt really wanted to emulate. He had been going to the Redmen's practice with his dad since he was three years old. He became a water boy as soon as they let him, and he kept the job until he could play in seventh grade.

"I know Dad was a great player here, and I know he went Division I," Colt said. "And I wanted to be around him. We try not to take it home. It comes up, though. I'm sure he knows how hard I work, and I hope he understands that I want him to be as proud of me as I am of him."

Colt paused. Then he stammered the way teenage boys have stammered for generations when they believe their fathers do not understand them. "Sometimes," he said, "I feel like it's hard for me to get that through to him."

It was time to dress for practice. Colt went inside the football complex and traded his bow tie and suspenders for a form-fitting T-shirt and padded football pants. He got his ankles taped and put his helmet in his lap and the scowl back on his face. In no time flat, Colt was focused, fierce, and ready to play like he was six feet tall.

Coach Barta was already in the middle of the locker room, leaning against the stand holding the video projector and holding a practice schedule with notes scrawled on the back. He had a lot on his mind and had already made a pair of big decisions. The first was that the quarterback rotation was over; Travis Rempe was going to lead the Redmen from here on out. He was more athletic than Ethan Eastes, and it was time to settle into some continuity on offense. Coach Barta called them in separately to tell them.

Almost immediately, a cocksure attitude that had been missing returned to Travis. He and his twin, Trevor, had long been local legends in town, known as double-barreled Dennis the Menaces who had once nearly burned down the Rempe homestead. Both were blond, and both were athletic, but the similarities stopped there. Travis was more reserved like his father, Bill, a linesman who balanced a quiet devotion to his family with a wry sense of wonder at how they had all managed to survive together. When his oldest daughter, Tabitha, decided to go to law school, Bill was dutifully proud of her but offered her some advice.

"You better be a good lawyer," he told her, "because either the boys are going to need you, or I am when I kill them."

Trevor was more of a free spirit like his mother, Stacy. She taught first grade and flung herself headlong into one activity or another. She headed the cheerleader squad and the dance team. She made sure the spirit signs were painted and posted throughout town. She taught religious instruction in the Catholic parish. During football games, she often let loose a warble that was somewhere between a yodel and a war cry and blistered the ears.

Like her, Trevor was a doer. He balanced his duties as a football captain with the lead and hammy role of Ellard, the not-so-bright redneck, in the school play, *Virgil's Family Reunion*. Most nights Trevor didn't get home until well past ten. The only time he did not have a smile on his face was on game day. He pasted a nasty look on his face after school and refused to talk to anyone.

Now he and Travis were the fullback and quarterback that Coach Barta had told their momma they'd become eighteen years ago.

Ethan, or "E," came out of Coach Barta's office the same way he went in: stoic. He was one of those quiet kids who are so stealthy that you could have tethered him to you on a two-foot rope and still forgotten he was there after fifteen minutes. E worked hard, was a fine athlete, and had a big heart. His little brother, Kale, had Down's syndrome and was a sophomore at the high school, and E doted on him.

E's father, Patrick, was a paramedic for the Smith County Emergency Medical Service, and E was hoping to get into firefighter school at Hutchinson County Junior College. He was not, however, a natural leader of men, and it had cost him the quarterback job.

Coach Barta had made a second decision that he wanted to pass on to his assistants. "We're going back to the old shirts," he said, matter-of-factly. "We haven't played worth a damn in the new ones."

Mike Rogers and Tim Wilson smiled at each other and then turned their faces quickly so as not to be caught. Coach Barta's superstitions had long been a source of amusement. The bottoms of the khaki Dockers he wore on game day were frayed. He wasn't going to change them, though; he had won a lot of ball games in those pants. Coach Barta had known better than to break the plastic on the new red polo shirts that had been purchased for the coaches for this season. There was nothing wrong with the old ones.

Big Hutch, who took everything Coach Barta said to heart

but nothing all that seriously, winked at the young assistants. He wasn't superstitious at all but knew that part of his job description was seconding his old friend's motion.

"I agree with you, Coach," he said. "I think those new shirts have caused the boys to fumble a lot. That's a heck of a coaching decision."

No one was smiling in the locker room now, however, as Coach Barta leaned against the video projector and glanced down at his notes. It was time to tune his team up, and he was prepared to pull out every motivational trick in his bag to do so.

"Now, you guys are lucky enough to have Coach Bill Snyder come here and talk to you for homecoming," Coach Barta said, referring to the former football coach at Kansas State University. "He's a good friend of mine, so make a point of shaking his hand and introducing yourself."

Snyder had been the coach who transformed an agricultural college with a dismal football history into a perennial power. When he was hired in 1989, the Wildcats were in the midst of a twenty-seven-game losing streak, had been to only one bowl game, and had captured one conference title in ninety-three years of play. When he retired in 2003 with a record of 136–68–1, Kansas State had won another conference title and six bowl games, had posted a perfect 11–0 season in 1998 to earn its first no. 1 ranking, and had produced thirty-three AP All-Americans, forty-two NFL draft picks, and forty-six first-team academic All-Americans. Among them were Coach Barta's son, Brooks, and Mark Simoneau.

Now, Snyder was demonstrating his high regard for Coach Barta and the Smith Center Redmen. He was climbing onto a plane Friday afternoon to fly to Smith Center to deliver the keynote address at the school assembly and to serve as grand marshal of the Old Settlers Day parade.

Coach Barta nodded to the freshmen to turn off the lights, and then switched the video projector on and watched the images of the Norton game flicker before his team.

"We should be better than we were last year," he said. "We don't have any confidence. Last year, I'd go out on the field on fourth and four, and those guys would tell me, 'Coach, don't worry.' When I went out the other night, nobody said anything to me.

"Let me show something," he said.

Coach Barta started with the offense and ran play after play on the screen. He went down each position and compared the current Redmen to last year's team.

"Left tackle," he said, referring to Justin. "It's the same guy we've had for the last two years. He's better than he was last year."

"Left guard, center, right side of the line," he called out, "Better, about the same, better and better."

He named all twenty-two positions and declared this year's team superior to the previous season's juggernaut in all but two areas: quarterback and defensive end, where Joe Windscheffel and Braden Wilson had played. In sixty seconds, Coach Barta performed an exorcism, casting out the domineering ghosts of Drew Joy, Grady Godsey, Matt Seemann, Kerby Rice—all of last year's senior class.

"You seriously should be confident," he said. "You have not lost a game. I was downtown the other day, and everybody was hanging their heads like we lost. You can be a great football team if you take care of each other and if you all want to be part of something special."

Coach Barta let the video sputter along in silence for another twenty seconds. "Remember, you all are special," he said.

---

For the remainder of the week, the Redmen growled as they bear-crawled beneath the blocking sled, and their pads popped furiously as they squared off in one-on-one tackling. During team drills, Travis Rempe worked on his ball-handling skills, carrying out his fake handoffs with conviction. His brother Trevor alternated plays with Joel Osburn at fullback, and each was exploding through the middle of the line and hitting linebackers whether they had the ball or not. At the water break, Kris Lehmann sat on the driver-side steps of the panel truck as streams of sweat wriggled down his face.

"This feels like a practice from last year," he said to Marshall, Colt, Justin, and Kalen Mace, who were squatting up against the truck in the shade. "I think we're getting there."

By Thursday, the night before their big game with the Phillipsburg Panthers, the Redmen were keyed up more than usual. A bonfire and pep rally awaited them after practice, as well as "the Snake," an unruly tradition where the kids piled into cars and pickups and engaged in water balloon and whipped cream fights as they swirled through town. I had been hearing about it for weeks—from the players, who breathlessly awaited its arrival, and from their parents, who stayed off the streets for the night and prayed that another year would go by without a major incident.

Fortunately, Smith Center's geography was compact— only 1.2 square miles—and I traveled it frequently with Mary and Jack, and we had become part of its commerce and community. We got our gas at the First Stop at the blinking yellow light at the intersection of Highways 36 and 281. We ate our double cheeseburgers and fries for $3.75, as well as paid for our weekly home trash pickup (nine dollars a month) at the Jiffy Burger. We bought Jack's John Deere toys at Orscheln Farm and Home, whose lumber and jeans, riding lawn mowers, and hardware targeted the modern farmer. The Dollar General Store and ALCO store faced each other across Highway 36 and were daily stops for the things you don't know you need until you need them, such as towels, corkscrew, outdoor grill, bulk toilet paper, televisions, and digital video recording disks, as well as for things we did not need, like jumbo packs of Twizzlers, whoopie cushions, and a magic wand.

We, along with the whole town, purchased our Redmen wear from Kathy McCary, who had started as a bus driver at the school before retiring as head of food services in 2002. She was the restless sort and had made her own clothes since she was a little girl, so it was a natural next step for her to start Third Street Designs. It was Kathy who was responsible for the ubiquitous red fleeces, T-shirts, hats, and blankets that were stamped with the Redmen logo.

As for Main Street itself, it had not fared well. The Coolidges' clothing store lasted until the late 1970s before vanishing for good. Dreiling's department store disappeared about the same time, and now was the location for the Hardly Used secondhand store. The Mini-Max—which Morse Boucher had run and where Joe Nixon had worked—closed in the mid-1990s.

Still, Smith Center had not yet surrendered. The town offered some remarkable facilities, like its public library and the Srader Center, where meeting rooms, basketball and racquetball courts, and a workout room drew people daily. Mary had been in and out of the fifty-bed Smith County Hospital in less than an hour after a fall necessitated six stitches from Dr. Joe Barnes, whose two sons played for the Redmen. Another day, it took the same amount of time for Jack, who had a high fever, to have blood drawn, his chest X-rayed and urine tested before being diagnosed with a bacterial infection by twenty-nine-year-old Dr. Justin Overmiller, who had also played for Coach Barta and had returned home after finishing his studies at the University of Kansas. Mary and I exercised most days at the adjacent Gardner Wellness Center, a state-of-the-art health club, as Dr. Barnes's wife, Arloa, a physical therapist, supervised the rehabilitation of the high school athletes and octogenarians under her care.

We went to the movies at the Center Theater, which showed first-run movies each night at seven thirty. Admission was only four dollars with an even better deal on Tuesday nights, when a ticket cost fifty cents less and came with free popcorn. We ate Kansas City strip steaks at Duffy's Tavern on Main and New York, where with a salad bar, a baked potato, and two beers the bill was still below eighteen dollars. We got our prescriptions filled at Family Healthmart. I got my hair cut at Paul's barbershop, which Paul Seemann, eighty years old, had first opened in 1963. His hands trembled a bit from a stroke four years ago, but they were stilled with a comb and razor in hand. I always looked better leaving his shop than I had when I came in.

How much we had become a part of this community became apparent to us as we cruised through town watching "the Snake" lurch along on the night before the homecoming game, music and laughter coming from one pickup truck after another as water balloons flew through the air. Something else was coming from the procession as well: shouts of "Jack" and "Joe" and "Mary." We stopped on Main Street to watch, and cars and trucks would veer out of line to come talk to us for a few minutes. We were talking with a group of Redmen crammed into Marshall's pickup when a Smith Center police officer pulled up behind us.

Marshall, Colt, Joe Osburn, and the Rempes all had their shirts off. Some were wearing bandanas on their heads. Each of their faces was flushed from laughing and the pure joy of teenage hijinks, of pelting each other and giving chase through town.

"Is there a problem?" the officer, a woman, asked.

"None at all," I told her. We exchanged smiles.

"They're just boys, and we let them have their fun for a night," she said. "We'll shut it down soon."

I was in no hurry for it to end. In fact, I was looking forward to homecoming and Old Settlers Day.

# 9

This is one play we're going to remember for the rest of our lives.
—Travis Rempe, September 26, 2008

Eldon Heinschel was pushing ninety years old but waved a strong hand in the direction of the thunderous applause coming from the grandstand. Because of the homecoming match-up with rival Phillipsburg and the balmy late September weather, Hubbard Stadium was jam-packed with three thousand people.

"They just honored a guy from the undefeated 1933 team," Coach Barta told his team. "That's what you want seventy-five years from now. You want to say 'I played on an undefeated championship team.'"

He let the notion hang there and walked to the back of the locker room. There was not much needed in the way of motivation; every year the showdown with "P-Burg" was widely anticipated. The Panthers had a tradition of athletic excellence in Class 3A, especially in basketball and volleyball. The two towns were only thirty miles away, and their kids had played baseball and wrestled, and struck up friendships. They went to each other's dances. In fact, Colt's girlfriend, Lexie, was from Phillipsburg. The fact that "P-Burg" hadn't beaten the Redmen since 2002 had brought the rivalry to full boil.

How much did Phillipsburg hate losing to the Redmen? Badly enough to turn against Tad Felts, the seventy-six-year-old news and sports director at the Phillipsburg-based radio station. For the past fifteen years, Tad's golden baritone has been the voice of the Redmen on KQMA on the FM dial. His choosing to call the Smith Center games over Phillipsburg's, and the station's decision to broadcast the Redmen on the more powerful FM airwaves, have not gone over well in town. Tad has been sneered at, yelled at, and even had his car vandalized. It matters little that since 1968 Tad has been up at four o'clock each morning preparing broadcasts and is on the road until well after midnight calling the basketball, volleyball, wrestling, and track contests of the area's schools, most of them in Phillipsburg.

"I sort of understand it," he told me. "Communities around here have a lot of pride, especially in their high schools. It's caused me some problems with a few people, but just a few. Besides, I wouldn't trade my forty years here for anything else. I've done literally thousands of games, and it never gets old. I'm the luckiest guy in the world."

This was supposed to be the year the Panthers took down the Redmen. They were physically bigger than the Redmen, thanks to a recent school consolidation that brought five very bruising football players to Phillipsburg from Eastern Heights High School, including the 225-pound fullback Ben Suchsland. The Redmen's uninspiring performance at Norton further buoyed the optimism coming out of Phillipsburg. Statewide, there were more doubts than ever about Smith Center's senior class, and that is exactly what

Brock Hutchinson wanted the Redmen to hear before they took the field against the Panthers.

"They are bigger, faster, and stronger than you," he told the team, stalking the front of the locker room.

Little Hutch truly appeared upset. He stabbed a finger at the back of the room where, on the other side of the coach's office in another locker room, the Panthers were getting their final pep talk.

"That's what they're telling them in there," he said. "And seniors, you are weenies, wimps, and wusses, and they are going to take you apart right here on your home field."

He stopped pacing, paused, and lowered his voice.

"There are two ways to play football, gentlemen," he said. "You respond and play, or you cower. This game does not have to be close. Big players make big plays. Remember that."

Then, Little Hutch leaned back like he was about to shimmy under a limbo bar, and roared loud enough for his face to turn red.

"WE ARE?" he screamed.

"REDMEN!" came the reply.

"WE ARE?" he asked again.

"REDMEN!" it came back again.

"WEEEEE ARRRRRRE?" he screeched.

"REDMEN!" echoed back, full-throated.

To the sound of crashing pads and slapping helmets, the team rushed through the door and out on the field and very nearly steamrolled the cheerleaders and children who held the banner they crashed through and formed the gauntlet they ran. They were jumping and pounding on each other as if they were on trampolines.

This newfound enthusiasm carried over to the first possession of the game. Colt took a handoff from Travis and squirted thirty-three yards to the Smith Center 49-yard line. On the next play, Joe Osburn skipped over a Panthers tackler at the line of scrimmage and slashed twenty more yards before being run out of bounds. Then Colt got the ball again and took it to the 4-yard line. Trevor banged it home. The drive took only five plays and two minutes to put the Redmen up, 6–0.

When the Panthers came onto the field for their first drive, they were poised and purposeful. They were, indeed, big boys, outweighing the Redmen's defensive front by an average of forty pounds. They were burying Trevor and Dillon Corbett at the line of scrimmage, and Ben Suchsland rumbled into the Smith Center secondary time and again. The Panthers put together a methodical sixteen-play, seven-and-a-half-minute drive that was capped when quarterback Dylan Frantz slung a rope to the sideline that wide receiver Chance Keiswetter caught in stride for an eighteen-yard touchdown. When Zach Wood kicked the extra point, the Redmen were actually down, 7–6.

"Let's run this one back," said Coach Barta, gathering his team as they came off the field.

He meant it. The Redmen were precisely coached, and nowhere was this more apparent than in their return game. Every return was set up for a naked reverse, which allowed time for the Redmen to set up a wall along the designated sideline and provide a lane for either Colt or Joe Osburn to motor through. It really was a thing of beauty to watch eight players gracefully loop to the sideline and then hammer defenders on their blind side. This return began with Joe Osburn catching the ball on the 1-yard line and then racing right, where he palmed the ball to Colt crossing behind him.

Except Joe kept his right arm tucked, found another gear, and sold the deception that he had the ball so well that the Panthers gave chase.

Colt, meanwhile, was scooting up the left sideline, and defenders were falling like dominos ahead of him as the Redmen were laying them out. At midfield, Colt zigged in and then out, so deftly that the final two Panthers took each other out. The whole team was racing along the sideline as Colt staggered into the end zone for a ninety-nine-yard touchdown return.

Leading the celebration was Trenton Terrill, who was using his braced knee to pole-vault himself down the field. Earlier in the afternoon at a school assembly, Trenton had been named the homecoming king. It was easy to see why. He was another straight-A student. Before he was crowned at the assembly, he climbed off the stage to join the Chansonaires—the school's elite vocal group—and performed.

Now, however, Trenton could not stop himself and nearly took an exhausted Colt out with an unintended chest pump. Both winced as they banged each other. The Redmen made the two-point conversion and were up, 14–7. When they held the Panthers on three plays and forced a punt, Coach Barta decided it was time to test his team and perhaps tear the heart out of Phillipsburg. They had run the ball up the middle three times and now were stalled at their own 27-yard line, facing a fourth down and one. Travis began to jog off the field as the punting team came on.

"Wait, wait," Coach Barta said, pulling the headset down from his mouth. "We're going for it."

He gave Travis the play, a fullback dive straight ahead, and as the Redmen quarterback returned to the field, fans from both sides came to their feet. The essence of Smith Cen-

Coach Roger Barta doing the Tad Felts radio show at the Second Cup Café.

The grain elevator at the south end of Smith Center stores the wheat, soybeans, and milo from Smith County and beyond.

A sign at the marker for the geographic center of the continental United States near Smith Center, Kansas.

Marshall McCall at the Pizza Hut for the traditional team dinner the night before a game.

Justin Nixon, a 350-pound lineman, had been a starter since his sophomore year and was hoping to be the first member of his family to attend college.

Defensive coordinator Brock Hutchinson leading the defensive walk-through the night before a game.

Colt Rogers, a five-foot-three, 135-pound running back, was the Redmen's leading rusher as well as an undefeated and two-time state champion in wrestling.

Colt's dad, Mike Rogers, was Smith Center's first high school All-American and went on to become a running back at the University of Kansas. He coaches running backs and special teams.

JACK KRIER

Senior running back Joe Osburn takes a pitch against the Norton Bluejays in what turned out to be the Redmen's closest game.

MARY KENNEDY

Smith Center High School principal Greg Koelsch (in white shirt, with necktie) watching the homecoming pep rally at the town's four-way stop.

As Smith Center's athletic director, Greg Hobelmann schedules games and referee crews, takes tickets, leads the student broadcast team, and coaches golf.

MARY KENNEDY

Coach Barta and the Redmen on the most eagerly awaited float of the town's annual Settlers' Day Parade.

Trevor, Stacey, Travis, and Bill Rempe at the last home game for Redmen seniors. Bill and Stacey wore the number of each of the twins.

Willie, Gavin, Jay, and Bill Overmiller on the farm their family has owned since the late nineteenth century. Jay played for Coach Barta; Willie is a junior running back; and Gavin, a fifth grader, is a team manager and a future Redman.

The Redmen cheerleaders get ready to welcome the team to the field.

Senior running back Joe Osburn struggled with his studies, but persevered to become one of the most explosive runners Smith Center had ever seen.

Trevor Rempe (8), Travis Rempe (9), Kris Lehmann (10), and Marshall McCall (29) lead the exultant Redmen onto the field after eliminating La Crosse from the state playoffs.

The NASA Lab, or "man cave," is the nerve center of Smith Center football. It is where Coach Barta and the staff scout opponents and set their game plans.

Trenton Terrill, Kris Lehmann, Trevor Rempe, and Marshall McCall—the four senior captains—on their way to receive the state championship trophy, Smith Center's fifth consecutive title, which ties a state record.

Tim Wilson, Brock Hutchinson, Marshall McCall, Coach Barta, Dennis Hutchinson, and Mike Rogers with the championship trophy. Tim, Brock, and Mike played for Coach Barta at Smith Center; Dennis (Big Hutch) has been his assistant for all thirty-one years.

The Redmen, their parents, and coaches circle up, as they do after all games. It's a time to celebrate and be grateful for their community.

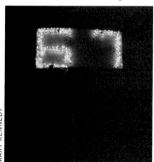

Smith Center's sixty-seven straight victories—a state record and the nation's current longest high school winning streak—are celebrated in Christmas lights and hoisted aloft by a forklift at Jones Machinery, which looms behind Hubbard Stadium.

ter football was simplicity, which was embodied by how Redmen quarterbacks called their signals. There were no fancy
number sequences or fancy shifts. On every play the two
ends, Kris Lehmann and Kalen Mace, were lined up inside to
make seven across on the line. Behind them, Travis was going
to hand the ball to either the fullback or one of the two running backs. Every so often, rarely actually, the quarterback
kept the ball. It was straight-up power football and was trig-
gered by Travis's simple command of "Down. Set. Go."

Hubbard Stadium was still as Travis reached underneath
Logan Tuxhorn. "Down. Set. Go." Only the crash of pads
could be heard as Joel Osburn, Joe's brother and a fullback,
bulled through the line for the first down.

Eight minutes later, the Redmen were in the end zone,
and twenty-four seconds after the ensuing kickoff they had
the ball back again, after the Panthers' quarterback Frantz
pitched the ball behind his running back on the sweep and
Kris Lehmann pounced on it at the 13-yard line. This time,
the Smith Center drive culminated with Marshall taking a
handoff up the middle for a 28–7 Redmen lead.

The Panthers didn't roll over, though. They took the ball
seventy-nine yards—forty-eight of them on a nifty run by
running back Derek Rowland—and at halftime the score
was Smith Center 28, Phillipsburg 14. The Redmen's locker
room was subdued, confident even, and Coach Barta did not
have much to say.

"That was the best half of football you guys have played,"
he told them. "Let's not mess around. Let's go out there and
put them away." On defense, the Redmen punished the
Panthers and held them scoreless in the third quarter. The
Panthers' offensive line was tiring under the quick and persistent assault of Trevor Rempe and Dillon Corbett. Logan

Tuxhorn was smashing running backs from the middle line-backer position. Colt was slashing underneath and collaring players twice his size. In fact, Colt was having one of his best games. He had a touchdown on the kickoff return and had gained eighty-three yards running the ball. He had a game-high twelve tackles as well.

In a span of a minute, however, he made a pair of mistakes that let the Panthers back in the game.

It was no secret that the Redmen had trouble holding on to the ball. On the second play of the fourth quarter, Colt took a handoff from Travis, spun out of a tackle around his neck, and lunged forward holding the ball out with one hand to try to gain an extra yard. Instead, he was hit, the ball squirted loose, and Phillipsburg recovered it.

On the sidelines, Mike Rogers grimaced and crouched to his knees. He was the running backs' coach and had spent the prior week putting the Redmen through fumble drills, reminding them they had to be more careful with the football. He had also made the mistake of reading the Kansas high school football message board, prepzone.com, which was maintained by the Topeka newspaper.

Mike wasn't alone. Brock was a frequent visitor to the site, and Coach Barta had even confessed to checking out what was being said there on occasion. It was a well-trafficked site, where posters mostly extolled the virtues of their hometown teams. The Redmen, however, inspired bitter passions, and the threads about them got mean and personal. Lately, the anonymous posters were rehashing familiar arguments: that Colt couldn't hang on to the ball, that he was only playing because his dad was a coach.

On the sidelines, Mike hung his head and did everything

in his power not to bark at his son. He kept his cool as the Panthers drove down to the Smith Center 35-yard line, and was rewarded for it when Cody Tucker snuffed out a screen pass and forced the Panthers to punt.

Colt, who also returned punts, dropped back to his own 10-yard line and watched as a booming kick sailed into the autumn night. Mike barked at Colt to stay away from it.

"Let it go," he said, betting the ball would bounce in the end zone and be brought out to the 20-yard line.

Instead, Colt backed up to the 2-yard line and followed the football into his arms. Only he dropped it. The ball bounced into the end zone. Colt went after it, but as soon as he picked it up, he was tackled in the end zone for a safety.

"Quit trying to make everything a damn home run," Mike yelled, meeting his son at the sideline.

Colt barked something unintelligible back through his mouthpiece. Mike's eyes blazed. He turned and walked the other way.

Now trailing 28–16 and with the ball, the Panthers took little time to march downfield, score, and pull within five points, 28–23, with a little more than five minutes to play.

"Marshall, you're in for Colt," Mike said as the Redmen offense took the field after the kickoff.

Marshall hesitated.

"Get in for Colt," Mike repeated. "Protect the football, and let's not try to get too fancy."

Colt was on the field and looked stunned when Marshall tapped him on the shoulder. He looked over at his dad.

"You're out," Mike said.

Big Hutch and Little Hutch glanced at each other.

"Mike," said Tim Wilson. Mike didn't answer.

Colt trotted off the field, went as far away from his father as he could get, and took off his helmet. He was through for the game.

The Rempes, however, were just getting started. On the first play from scrimmage, Travis handed the ball to Trevor, who creased through the hole opened by Logan Tuxhorn and bounced right for forty-one yards to the Phillipsburg 39-yard line. Twice more, Trevor banged inside but only for a couple of yards. On third down and ten, Travis faked a handoff to Trevor and then followed Marshall around the right end for twenty yards and a Redmen first down on the 15-yard line. Trevor was there to yank him up by his face mask, and the twins pounded on each other as they have ever since they were little.

Travis, however, had learned something from the Norton game. He knew his team had a tendency to get too emotional. Before he called the next play, he looked around the huddle.

"Deep-breathe on three," he commanded.

The Redmen looked at each other.

"One, two, and three," Travis counted.

They breathed deep. They exhaled.

"It works," said Marshall, smiling.

When Trevor rumbled ten yards for a first and goal on the Panthers' 5-yard line, it looked like the Redmen were going to put their rivals away. Instead, Phillipsburg stiffened. Trevor ran into the middle of the line three times, and three times he could not get in the end zone. Coach Barta called a time-out. When he met his offense on the field, he was pleased at what he saw. They were smiling, and talking at once, trying to tell him what play they wanted to run.

"We're taking it in, Coach," Marshall said.

Coach Barta turned and headed for the sideline. Travis called for his team to gather around him. He grabbed his brother's hand and was almost giggling. He was the starting quarterback, and this was his team. He waited for Marshall and Joe and the linemen to clasp hands.

"This is one play we're going to remember for the rest of our lives," he said. "Now, let's knock them on their asses. On one."

It was quiet again when Travis leaned over Logan.

"Down," he said. "Set. Go."

Travis gave his brother the ball, and this time Trevor's whole body crossed the goal line. The Redmen had sent the Panthers back up Highway 36 with another defeat.

———

There were horses and midget go-carts and dozens of antique John Deere tractors refurbished to vintage glory, their two-cylinder engines making the unmistakable syncopation that had earned them the nicknames of "Johnny Poppers" throughout rural America. The volunteer fire department and semitrucks, convertibles, and pickups wiggled down the parade route. Candy flew out their windows to the children who lined Main Street. Members of the Rotary Club, the Lions, and the VFW walked by, and the marching band played.

The biggest applause came when the school floats passed. The junior high volleyball girls were on one, and the high school's Lady Reds were on another. The Redmen in training, the seventh and eighth graders, wore their red jerseys and rode on a small flatbed. The Redmen donned their white jerseys and lined both sides of a huge flatbed. Justin and his brother Josh were smart enough to bring lawn chairs and towered above the rest of the team. The whole team was bright-eyed and tossed candy and smiles to the grade schoolers who trailed along after them. Most of the seniors had visited the elementary school earlier in the week and signed the trading cards that bore their names and likenesses.

The paraders, as well as the paradegoers, congregated at the four-way stop. There was a barbecue set up, and the high school students went through the line first. Justin had his plate piled high with burgers and hot dogs. Marshall, Kris Lehmann, and the Rempes accepted kind words. Colt was there, too. He was sheepish about the fumbles and the run-in with his father.

Colt was not nearly as sheepish, however, as Mike Rogers was the following night, when he met his fellow coaches in the NASA Lab to break down game film of their next opponent, the Ellis Railers. Brock, Big Hutch, and Tim Wilson let him have it.

They reminded him that Colt was the team's best player and that his mistakes were made because he was trying too hard. By the time Coach Barta arrived, Mike was hanging his head.

"You don't have to say anything, Coach," Mike said. "Brock and Tim have already chewed me out."

Mike knew that he deserved the scolding. He had felt awful as soon as he pulled Colt from the game on Friday night. At home afterward, he apologized to his son. Mike told him that he had been listening to the wrong people: the anonymous Internet posters and other jealous parents.

"I got caught up in what other people were saying and thinking," he told Colt, "instead of having faith in the people I love and trust. It won't happen again."

The following day Coach Barta put the incident to rest for good during a film session for the team. Mike was in

Phillipsburg with the junior varsity, and the varsity was watching a replay of their victory over the Panthers. When the Phillipsburg punter dropped back on the fateful play, Coach Barta paused the tape.

"Colt, you want me to play this twelve or thirteen times?" he asked, his eyes remaining fixed to the screen.

"Oh, no, Coach," Colt answered.

"You know your dad is a hard ass and believes if you fumble you don't play, don't you?" he said. He waited a beat.

"And you guys thought I was tough," he said.

There was laughter, and then Coach Barta fast-forwarded the tape past the play. No one was ever going to watch it again.

# PART THREE

# THE CUTTING

# 10

It ain't bragging if you do it.
　　　　　　　　　　—Jack Benn, October 3, 2008

We are a digital society, one with a great deal of time on our hands, and the proof of it is in our Twitters and BlackBerrys and cell phones. I was surprised, however, how deeply the new culture had reached into rural America. Our home was wireless. Travis Rempe and several Redmen had pages on Facebook. In the locker room, in the library, and at the Pizza Hut, cell phones buzzed and vibrated with text messages, the preferred mode of communication for teenagers everywhere.

It was the prepzone.com message board on the Internet site of the *Topeka Capital-Journal*, however, that demonstrated how tangled we are in instant articulation. Over twenty years as a sportswriter, I've learned how passionate folks are about the games, pastimes, and teams they follow. I'm also tech-savvy enough to understand that the Internet has taken sports talk from bar rooms and talk radio and put it in our homes and offices twenty-four hours a day. But who knew how consuming, and often how rancorous, the devotees of high school football talk in northwest Kansas were?

It was the afternoon after the Redmen dispatched Phillipsburg and Ellis ran over Hoxie, 49–14, that a thread began on prepzone.com with the subject line "Smith Center vs. Ellis." The Railers were undefeated at 4–0, talented, and the latest hope to end the Redmen's winning streak.

Statetitle, one of the site's nearly five thousand members, teed up the discussion with this initial post: "Think this is the week it ends," he wrote. "Hopefully there are at least a few others who think this."

They were off from there, in fragmented sentences, misspelled names, and twisted logic. Some of them posted and responded during business hours. Others were night owls. Many were like me and the Smith Center coaching staff—voyeurs and eavesdroppers.

"We all need to realize that smith center just might be the most overrated team in the state this year due to the success of last years team," wrote railer.

RedmenI didn't think so, though he was in the minority. "Sure it was last years seniors as well as three classes of seniors before them that started the streak," he wrote, identifying himself as a parent of one of last year's seniors. "Any of the seniors last year would tell you in all seriousness that their toughest games last year were played every single night at practice. That speaks volumes for the talent and work ethic of the current players. I'm very proud of this year's team for having been patient playing in the shadows of last year's boys and now having additional pressure put upon them to continue the streak."

The thread went on for a week with more than three hundred posts, viewed by almost four thousand members.

One poster, Coyote Ugly, was a parent of a player from Weskan, a tiny town in far west Kansas where the kids play eight-man football. It also was the former home of Joe, Joel, and Jon Osburn, who had come to Smith Center the previous season when their father, Robert, was hired as a math teacher.

The Osburns had nine kids, six of whom were adopted. Those numbers were coveted by rural school districts trying to hold on across Kansas. The fact that Joe, Joel, and Jon were good athletes spawned many rumors about Smith Center's recruiting, as well as jealousy from towns near and far.

"Those boys learned a lot of their football in Weskan, where they played 4 years," Coyote Ugly wrote. "No doubt they have improved while at SC, because of the great program they have in effect there. I guess our season, like only having 11 boys suited Friday, then having a tailback with a giant cast having trouble holding the ball, but having no other choice to play, is getting to me."

The Osburns had been a gift to Redmen football. Jon Osburn was growing into the system and would likely start the following year on defense. Joel Osburn was the second-strongest player on the team after Justin Nixon. He was six feet, two inches and 210 pounds of pure muscle. He squatted over five hundred pounds, benched more than three hundred pounds, and enjoyed the weight room. Still, the coaches could not get Joel to run with his shoulders square to the ground and with power. He ran straight up, giving tacklers an ample target. Joel was conscientious but a work in progress for the junior colleges and small colleges recruiting him.

Joe, though, was the more finished on-field prospect. As a running back, he had ankle-breaking moves and gear-shifting speed. With a dip of his shoulder, Joe made opponents look terrible as they dove for air long after he had run past. He also required a lot of work off the field.

In early October, Coach Barta called Joe to his office for a tête-à-tête. He had just gotten the first academic reports of the school year, and Joe was flunking a class. Joe's teachers told the coach that Joe was a capable student; he just was not handing in his work. At the same time, Joe was evolving into a major contributor for the Redmen. He was averaging more than eleven yards a carry and had nine tackles from his cornerback position against Phillipsburg. Coach Barta decided there was no use trying to light a fire under Joe; he recognized that he was fragile. Instead, he explained to Joe that he was not going to play if he was failing a class.

"That will hurt you plenty, but it's really not fair to your teammates," Coach Barta said. "They count on you."

Joe sat there impassively.

"Have you asked your teachers for help?" the coach asked.

Joe shrugged.

"Everyone around here wants you to succeed," he said. "You decide what you want to do. Either do the work, or don't play football. It's up to you."

---

No one needed to read message boards at the Second Cup Café. The As the Bladder Fills Club talked Redmen football in the mornings, the players' parents talked about it at lunch, and, in the evening, the teenage girls took the wait shifts and kept everyone up to date on what was going on over at school. The Second Cup had the best food in town, whether it was the fried eggs, bacon, and thick and buttered Texas toast for breakfast, or the taco salad that was a staple of the Mexican lunch special, or the barbecue plate at night. There is no place in New York (or any other big city) that offers a trio of brisket, pulled pork, and chicken wings, with a macaroni salad, green beans, and pudding for the bargain price of $7.18.

Lynn Pickel owned the place and did most of the cooking. Her husband, Craig, bred and trained German shorthair pointers, which accounted for the portrait prints of the hunting dogs on the wall. Lynn had an all-women staff that was good humored and plugged in to the high school. Julie Zabel's daughter, Kiley, was a junior. Meribeth Lambert's son, Grant, played fullback on the seventh grade team. Stephanie Favinger, a junior, had a little brother, Curtis, on the Redmen.

The women of the Second Cup Café followed and fed the Smith Center students. They extended these maternal feelings to their adult customers as well. They were always the first to know, for example this week, that Joe Osburn needed to buckle down in school, or that Colt's procedure to widen his esophagus had gone well but he was going to miss a couple of days of practice.

It was the As the Bladder Fills Club that really chewed over the football talk in the mornings. And in the week leading up to the Ellis game, no one was certain whether the Redmen had turned a corner in their victory over Phillipsburg.

"I'll tell you what," said Ivan Burgess. "I saw three of the hardest hits I have ever seen in high school football the other night."

"That big old Justin Nixon ties up two or three blockers, and it allows Logan Tuxhorn and the other linebackers to just tee off on those ball carriers," said Dick Stroup. "It isn't hardly fair."

Despite the bravado, a hint of doubt remained, and it wasn't limited to the denizens of the Second Cup Café. Some parents, and even some players, felt something was missing with this team. The town was starting to feel the weight of winning fifty-eight consecutive games.

There were only two people I came across in town who acted as if they were completely oblivious to the streak.

The first was Coach Barta, who never mentioned it and deftly sidestepped questions about it. When reporters asked him what he would do when the Redmen finally lost and the streak was over, he stopped them in their tracks with a simple response: "We'll start another streak."

Coach Barta knew that someday the streak would end, but he decided to treat it as he did all unanswerable questions such as mortality. What is the use of talking and thinking about the inevitable when all it is going to do is distract you from what you're doing right now?

The other person in town who seemed unfazed by the winning streak was Jack Benn. Jack loved football, and he believed totally that Coach Barta was a great leader and had been among the first in town to invest in the coach's philosophy of "getting a little bit better every day" as the best prescription for leading your life. Jack had watched the philosophy succeed in 1978 when Coach Barta took over his son's team, which was not very talented. In the coach's first year, the Redmen went 3–6, but played hard and with heart. The following year, the Redmen played for, and lost, their first championship game.

Jack also was considered the town's most knowledgeable Redmen watcher. He had multiple victories in the *Smith*

*County Pioneer*'s weekly contest where readers picked the winners of the local high school and college games. When Ivan Burgess wanted to pass on a reasoned football opinion to the readers of the *Echo*, he quoted Jack. With Ellis coming to town, this was one of those times. The Railers were one of nine undefeated teams left in Kansas's Class 2A, and since losing to the Redmen, 62–0, the previous season, the Railers had won ten of their last eleven games.

Earlier in the week, the *Hays Daily News* had written about how the Railers had been waiting for the trip to Smith Center, even posting stories about the Redmen's winning streak and run of four straight titles inside their weight room as motivation.

"Anyone we play would consider it a successful season if the only team they beat was Smith Center," said Ivan. "How about Ellis, Jack, they going to get us?"

Jack made a show of pondering the question, so he could command the whole table's attention.

"If you're going to get us, you got to get us early in the season, when the guys are getting used to each other, and we haven't found our timing," he said. "We were vulnerable early this season especially, having to replace those twelve seniors."

Heads nodded in agreement.

"Nobody is going to get us this year," Jack said. "It's too late. We're getting better every day."

Ivan smiled and pulled his dime store notebook from his front pocket. As he scrawled down some notes, he said, "That's why people criticize us in Smith Center for bragging."

"It ain't bragging if you do it," answered Jack.

Ivan's smile got wider. He wrote furiously in his notepad.

The pep rallies had lacked fervor so far this year, but Mike Rogers made sure that was about to change. He pulled a copy of the story about Ellis that had appeared in the Hays paper. Mike was not a pulpit pounder like Brock, but between a deadpan delivery and a look of shocked disbelief, he sold the words of the Ellis coach and players as major displays of disrespect.

"In the summer, Ellis head coach Butch Hayes and his players discussed opening the season 4–0 before a big Week 5 contest against Smith Center," he began reading.

"'It was a big goal,' junior running back Dylan Pfeifer said. 'We thought we would have a better chance at this game if we were going into it 4–0.'"

Mike looked up for dramatic effect. He glanced over at the team, many of whom he knew were hearing about Ellis's public pronouncements for the first time.

He continued: "'I think right now, there are a lot of teams out there that want to end that streak that Smith Center has,' Hayes said. 'We are no different. It would be an exciting thing to do.'"

Mike read the next part slowly, letting the implied insult sink in.

"This season, Smith Center has been tested far more than its record-breaking 2007 season where the Redmen featured nine college football signees, set several state records and outscored opponents 844–20. Led by senior offensive tackle Justin Nixon and junior halfback Colt Rogers (641 rushing yards), the Redmen have outscored their opponents 163–51 this fall, including a 22–20 win over Norton in Week 3. Phillipsburg also played Smith Center close last Friday."

Once more, Mike looked up. He read the following slowly and with the loud and correct ennunciation of a Shakespearean actor.

"'A lot of us watched film Tuesday night and they are not near the same team as they were, so we are going into this game thinking we know we can beat them,' Pfeifer said."

The boos and hisses came on cue. The table was set.

When the team filed from the gym into the common room for their pregame salad, lasagna, and garlic bread, they were even quieter and grimmer-faced than usual. They ate quickly and in silence, then headed to the football complex to prepare for their date with the Railers in three and a half hours. Of all the Redmen rituals, the one that amazed me most, and probably took the most discipline, was the team's complete and utter dedication to repose before a game. They were deadly serious about embracing utter serenity and visualizing how the game was going to unfold.

At home especially, the locker room looked like nap time at preschool. The lights were kept low, and bodies formed a checkerboard on the floor. Some slept, some fidgeted and stretched, and others bobbed and pulsated to the iPods in their ears. The coaches' office frequently looked the same, but a more apt description would be the recreation room of a nursing home. Coach Barta, Big Hutch, and Mike had no compunction about putting their heads on a pile of pillows. Tim Wilson mostly sat quietly or found a sliver of light to read by. Brock, on the other hand, was everywhere and nowhere. He was always in motion—stalking from one room to the next, working some Skoal over on his lower lip, anything to make the waiting go faster.

By the time kickoff rolled around, Coach Barta was relaxed and matter-of-fact with his team. He delivered what would be the shortest pregame talk of the season. "It's the fifth games of seasons that upsets usually happen—look it up," he said, fabricating statistics again. "We worked you hard this week. We haven't shut anybody out this year, and that is not acceptable. The goal is to put a zero on the scoreboard."

There was little doubt that the Redmen were going to do as they were told. On their opening drive, Travis, Trevor, Colt, and Joe split sixteen carries and drove eighty-nine yards down to the Railers 4-yard line. It nearly took the whole quarter, and now they faced fourth down and less than a yard to go. The combination of a botched handoff and guard Dillon Corbett slipping at the line of scrimmage resulted in Trevor falling an inch short of the first down. The Redmen might have come away empty on the scoreboard, but they had manhandled Ellis all the way downfield, and the Railers knew it.

The Railers did not celebrate their goal-line stand; they limped back to the offensive huddle, tired and relieved. Marshall gathered the defensive unit at the 10-yard line.

"Deep-breathe on three," he said. "One, two, three."

Marshall had felt his team coming together the previous week. He and Kris had spoken with Joe Osburn and had helped him sort out his studies. In practice, Marshall was seeing the little stuff, which made him believe the Redmen were becoming brothers. Justin tossed the water bottles to Van Tucker and Jesse and Kaden Roush, underclassmen who were pushing him and the other lineman hard in practice, instead of demanding water from the freshmen. Colt took a teeth-jarring hit in practice from Dereck McNary and then patted the sophomore on the helmet.

"No first downs, no points," Marshall said. "Do your jobs. Trust each other. We stop them talking right here."

For the next forty minutes, the Redmen did not look like the same team they had been the previous four weeks. Instead, they looked like last year's team. They took a 16–0 lead into halftime, and the "mercy" clock began running in the fourth quarter as the Redmen were leading, 40–0. Ellis not only had lost all illusions of being able to beat Smith Center, but quit trying after the first quarter. The Railers managed only 51 yards on the ground, while the Redmen ran for 405 yards and held the ball for nearly two-thirds of the game.

The best thing about the performance was that the Redmen sideline was perfectly calm throughout. The players did not look surprised or thrilled that they were taking apart what was supposed to be a good team. They played precisely as if they had expected to deliver a methodical and crushing defeat.

With five minutes left in the game, the junior varsity was moving the ball on the Railers. Marshall, Justin, the Rempes, and all the seniors were on the sideline with their helmets off and done for the evening.

"It feels like last year, doesn't it?" asked Travis to no one in particular. "They're just waiting for the horn to sound so they can go home."

"No, it's better than that," said Marshall, "because we're the ones who made them feel that way."

# 11

Little boys grow up wanting to be Redmen, and Redmen grow up to be champions.

        —Jay Overmiller, October 10, 2008

Jay Overmiller was weeks behind bringing in his soybeans. There was nothing he could do about the rain, though. For weeks it had been soaking his family's three thousand acres morning, noon, and night. He could not risk getting his combine stuck in a muddy field, and wet beans weren't worth cutting anyway. Weather was the master of farm life, and the Overmillers had been slaves to it on these plains since 1882, when Jay's great-grandfather had given each of his six sons a farm here. Instead of worrying about the work he had not gotten done, Jay put six hundred miles on his pickup this week going to ball games.

On Monday he was in Ellis watching his oldest son, Willie, gain fifty-eight yards on three carries from fullback and score a touchdown in the junior varsity's 52–0 rout of the Railers. On Thursday he was in WaKeeney watching his middle son, Trevor, play a junior high school game. Now, on Friday night, he was in Colby, a town of 5,500 in far west

Kansas, waiting for the Redmen to take on another pretty good team, the 4–1 Eagles, this time from Class 4A.

"I'm having a good week," Jay said with a toothy smile as he walked into the empty stadium, hours before game time.

Back in the late 1970s, Jay had been the first Redman to get noticed far beyond Smith Center. One of the national magazines had even singled him out as one of the best prospects in all of Kansas. On offense, Jay could get to holes quickly and carry his speed downfield. On defense, he got to opposing running backs even faster and blew them to bits with his strength. Jay's on-field exploits brought big-time recruiters to town.

He thought that he had died and gone to heaven when Tom Osborne, the iconic head coach of the University of Nebraska, wrote him letters. The Overmillers' land was seven miles south of the Nebraska state line, and Jay was a big Cornhusker fan.

Jay also was something of a reckless country boy. He worked hard on the farm, but he also liked to rodeo, and his specialty was riding bulls. He wasn't supposed to be playing football and competing in rodeos, but he got away with it for a while. During the second game of his junior season, however, Jay took a handoff and bounced it outside for a big gain before getting creamed by a tackle that mangled the outside of his right knee. This was before orthopedics could make a torn-up knee like new, and when surgery meant a scar from "ass to ankle." Jay's knee never fully recovered from the surgery, and he didn't help things. He kept riding bulls and deteriorating it more.

That season was the first year the Redmen made it to the state title game under Coach Barta, but Jay stood on the sideline in his street clothes. Jay returned for his senior season, but he was a step or three slower. Still, he can remember every single play of every game.

"I was not the player I once was," he said. "I was like a truck with one bad wheel. The college coaches disappeared. But, man, it was one of the best years of my life. I loved football. Still do."

Jay never turned bitter about the bad turn, and he credited Coach Barta for that. He was a sophomore when the coach came to Smith Center, and was immediately taken by his message of living for something other than oneself. Much as his sons' football games now served as his social hour, playing for the Redmen had taught him about social values. When his knee blew out and the college coaches went away, Coach Barta told Jay that was when he and his teammates needed each other most.

"Coach told me winning and scholarships were nice, but that wasn't what he wanted our football team to be about," Jay said. "He told me I had a chance to set the standard, be the example of sacrificing for each other, for being part of something bigger. He said playing football was easy, but living for others is a lot harder.

"I may not have been as good as I was before the knee injury, but before each game, when we walked on the field holding hands, I was as focused and committed as I had ever been to anything in my life," he went on. "The guys knew I was laying it down for them. We were brothers. It gave me confidence. It also taught me that real success is about love and respect."

After graduation, Jay taught himself about computers and went into the family farming business. He married his wife, Donna, who taught English at the junior high school.

Jay was among the first around here to get into precision farming. He had helped create computer programs for farmers. Each morning, he was up at dawn and in his pickup truck for the twenty-minute drive to his parents' house. The house was built in 1905, and his father, Bill, was born there.

Jay was impossibly sunny. He also was so good with his hands that other farmers hired him to repair and modify equipment. He kept a tight watch on his inventory so he could buy parts and fertilizer in bulk and at discounts. Jay's guilt about wandering from football game to football game this week was lessened because he had gambled and held on to last year's soybeans, and it had paid off. He had recently sold them at a premium of fifteen dollars a bushel. Jay was also buoyed by the precipitous drop in oil prices under way, which had brought down the cost of fertilizer.

Jay cherished his family time, and much of it revolved around the family business. Willie, Trevor, and even eleven-year-old Gavin were proficient at farmwork and drove tractors and grain carts from sunup to long after sundown. His daughter, Brittany, had done her share as well and now was a freshman at Washburn University. Jay was especially proud of her for finding a job at a bank in Topeka on her own to help with school expenses.

The best times for Jay, however, were playing cards with his kids at night or taking them hunting. They shot pheasants and quails and turkeys and, on the first day of deer season, played hooky from work and school to stalk the bucks they had spent the rest of the year dodging in their trucks at night. Brittany was arguably the most dead-eyed in the family, and Donna Overmiller made a stew from a deer's heart that was a delicacy.

Jay tried to get to every music recital, school pageant, and athletic event and by his count had managed to do so on all but three occasions. He did not even try to conceal the pure joy that he was experiencing watching his boys make their way through the Redmen football program.

"I used to drop in on Coach from time to time when I needed help on something," Jay said, "or to just tell him I still think about what he taught me."

Willie Overmiller is his father's son. He was ready immediately to join Jay and his grandfather in the family business. He spent all his off hours working with them. Until he finished high school, however, he intended to set his animal traps and catch raccoons, hunt for birds and deer, and play football—a game that he loved as much as his father did. He had Jay's low center of gravity and steamrolling power, but he was not very fast. He was only a sophomore, though, and was already playing special teams on the varsity and performing well on the junior varsity. Trevor, an eighth grader, was long and lean and a gifted athlete. He played tailback and safety. Basketball, however, was his first love.

Gavin was likely to be the greatest Redmen of all the Overmillers. Like all youngest sons, he was benefiting from the knowledge and toughness being handed down from his older brothers. But Gavin also had an outsized charisma. Everyone in town knew who Gavin was, and he in turn paid attention to what was going on around him. Moreover, he already had an unwavering belief in himself.

"Little boys grow up wanting to be Redmen, and Redmen grow up to be champions," Jay said. "We've said that around here for a long time. Gavin really believes that, and he already sees that for himself. He can envision himself being a star."

Gavin was already a water boy and one of the most conscientious of them all. He took seriously the orders handed down from the team trainer and manager, Leo Tuxhorn. Even ten steps slower than in his prime and hard of hearing, Leo retained his knack for communicating with young people. You could see how he had inspired so many people to join the army by the way he handled his young charges. He demanded precision and regimentation, and he made them know how important they were to the team. Leo also was the first to rub them on their heads and tell them what a good job they were doing.

When they were not toting water or picking up towels, Gavin and his fellow water boys were running plays and hurling the football around on the sidelines. All the water boys wanted to grow up to be Redmen, and you could almost see them six years from now on the field and hoisting a championship trophy in the air. Each of them already knew most of the Redmen playbook and called the plays just as they heard them. Gavin was a natural leader and played quarterback. He had a strong arm and a good turn of foot, and he was a big kid—not overweight but built like a fireplug with Popeye arms. Gavin had earned the nickname "Meat Wagon" from members of the team because of his size as well as his appetites. Beef jerky, hamburgers, hot dogs—Gavin was a carnivore.

As the kickoff of the Colby game was nearing, however, Gavin had left the sidelines to find his father. He still wanted to grow up and be a Redman. He still wanted to be a champion. Right now, however, he wasn't feeling well. All he wanted was a hug from his dad.

Jay gave him a long one.

The Redmen, meanwhile, were wandering the streets of

Colby, Kansas, or at least it felt like it. Outside of Smith Center, not much planning or comfort went into the locker rooms for visiting teams in western Kansas. The Hubbard football complex had lockers and showers for a visiting team of forty, but this was the exception. So far this season, the team had dressed and met in three-stall bathrooms and a junior high gymnasium. In Colby, the Redmen were led behind the concession stand and through a trail in the trees and into a corrugated tin workshop. It had a greasy garage floor, power saws, worktables, and a five-foot fan that sounded like a plane taking off. In the middle there even was a hamster, twirling the treadmill in his cage.

Someone said it was the school district's agriculture shop, but it was so dim, grimy, and overcrowded with power tools that it might as well have been a torture dungeon. There was a small lunchroom, and wave after wave of Redmen went in there to pad up. The looks on their faces as they searched for an inhabitable place to sit ranged from disbelief and amusement to plain old grossed-out. Coach Barta tried to turn the situation into a positive, but as he competed to be heard over the fan he just got more irritated.

A few moments earlier, Kris Lehmann and Colt Rogers had to tell Coach Barta that they had ridden the bus two and half hours across Kansas without their game jerseys. They had been slow packing up their gear back in Smith Center, and the coach had gone into the locker room and told them to hurry up and get on the bus. In their panic to get out, they had forgotten their white away jerseys. Both looked at the floor as they told the coach of their mistake. Thirty years ago, even fifteen years ago, Coach Barta would have benched his captain and star running back and let them hear about how they had let their team down. These days, he was older and far mellower. He let Kris and Colt know that he was disappointed, told them to stop by the office next week to talk about it, but ultimately let them borrow the jerseys of injured teammates and play.

Being trapped with a hamster in a noisy industrial workshop certainly did not improve the coach's mood. Colby had a new and young coaching staff, and had been eager to return the Redmen to its schedule after a six-year absence. Would it have killed them to provide nicer accommodations?

"Look around you, guys," he bellowed to be heard. "This should make you grateful for what we have at home."

Coach Barta's statement ricocheted off the tin and into the dark, which set off even more noise as his team leaned in and shifted to hear what their coach had just said. He threw his hands up and waved his team out the door. The sun was still shining, and out the Redmen came, squinting, shielding their eyes with their arms. They gathered in the shade under a tree, and Coach Barta remained at a loss for words.

"Guys, I understand gamesmanship, but this is not the way you're supposed to treat people," he said. "We play our games on the field. Let's go out and warm up a little. We'll figure something out."

As the Redmen killed time with languid warm-ups, Greg Hobelmann and his Smith Center video crew were setting up a broadcast operation far superior to most local cable-access channels. In fact, Greg had just gotten word that his self-taught band of students and adults, which included the pastor of one of the town's largest churches, had been selected to produce and broadcast the statewide live telecast of the Class 2A championship—whether the Redmen made it to the title game or not.

Greg was like a duck in the water. He seemed to glide through the day with a big smile and an air of serenity. Below the waterline, however, his fingers paddled his Treo frantically as he raced from the elementary school to take money at the door for the junior high volleyball game and then back to Hubbard Stadium to meet the referees for the junior high football game. Already this week, Greg had been to Ellis with the junior varsity on Monday, back in the Smith Center gym on Tuesday for volleyball matches, and to Wa-Keeney for league meetings.

He had four kids of his own. Alex, his oldest, was a freshman at Smith Center High School and played quarterback on the junior varsity and guard on the basketball team, and he was one of the best golfers in the state as well. Alyssa was a seventh-grade volleyball and basketball player. Allyson and Austin were fifth and third graders and made all the trips with their dad in preparation for their future careers in Smith Center sports.

It was the broadcast team, however, that Greg enjoyed the most. He built it from nothing by talking Nex-Tech, the local cable company, into lending the school some equipment and then welcoming all comers to learn how to work a camera, mix a soundboard, or run instant replay. They showed up at games before the Redmen and usually stayed long after them, breaking down their equipment.

I had driven the district Suburban to Colby so Greg could sit in the backseat with a pair of juniors, Christian Gretzschel and Robbie Hoffert, to diagram and explain how to set up the main broadcast board. Greg had vowed to bring as professional a production staff as possible to the state championship game. He also understood that it was a way to keep the few boys who were not athletically inclined invested in the high school.

It was high-tech and important work, and as soon as each game was over, it aired on tape delay on Channel 17 and was rerun throughout the week. The telecast offered enthusiastic play-by-play and commentary from John Terrill, Trenton's father, and Don Wick, a junior high school teacher and coach here for thirty years. They were going to be replaced on the championship broadcast by professional talent, but they were as proud as Greg that the kids had been recognized and were getting a star turn on live TV.

Christian and Robbie had puzzled over the wires and plugs for more than an hour. Finally, they believed they had the equipment broadcast-ready.

Greg flipped some switches and hit some buttons.

"You did it," he told them as the monitors came to life. "Good job."

Christian and Robbie beamed.

"We're ready for state," said Christian.

Kickoff was nearing, and Coach Barta refused to take his team back to the work shed. Instead, he herded them off the field to the parking lot where the buses sat. It was getting dark enough that players could slip into the trees to urinate without too many folks noticing. The Redmen were huddled between their two buses, and, across the field, the Colby grandstands were filled to capacity.

"Look at that, guys," Coach Barta said, pointing at the packed stands. "They're here for you. We've got a reputation out here in western Kansas. People pay good money to come see our dog-and-pony show. Let's not disappoint them. Make them quit early."

Another one of the Redmen's rituals was a chant borrowed from a Native American prebattle ceremony. Here in Colby, the team performed it with a mixture of show business enthusiasm and genuine ferocity. They ran to the middle of the field and formed a circle with the four captains in the center.

"*Na na naka toi yah,*" Marshall, Kris, Trenton, and Trevor yelled, bouncing in four separate directions until they reached their teammates for a flying chest bump.

"*Na na naka toi yah,*" the team answered back.

"*Como te, como te*" came next, and the circle would tighten by a few steps.

"*Na na naka toi yah.*"

"*Na na naka toi yah*" echoed back.

"*Como te, como te.*" The circle tightened again.

This went on until the Redmen were in a tight cluster, jumping, banging, and roaring at each other. In the past, this was the Indians' way of saying this is our land, and we're going to protect it. Now it was the Redmen's way of saying that they had no away games, that they owned the football field wherever it was they played.

The Colby Eagles quit throwing footballs and limbering up. They were transfixed as they watched from their sidelines. You could have heard a pin drop despite the massive crowd.

The Eagles quit right then and there, and the Redmen gave them an old-fashioned beating. It was excruciating to watch because the Colby players seemed to have little desire to be there.

Little Ethan Eastes delivered bone-jarring tackles—nine of them solo—and the Redmen defense forced eight punts as they held the Eagles to just 121 total yards. On offense, the Redmen scored at will. Colt scooted for 166 yards, Trevor for 62, Marshall for 60, Joe Osburn for 48, and Joel Osburn for 40.

The score was 20–0 in the opening minutes of the third quarter and 40–0 when the running clock finally ran out. The Redmen's celebration, however, was muted. They had expected to demolish the Eagles.

"We're 0 and 0 now," Marshall said, banging the shoulder pads of his teammates as they gathered for a postgame prayer.

"Preseason is over," said Trevor Rempe. "Now is what counts."

The Redmen were 6–0 and once more the Mid-Continent League champions. Their winning streak stood at sixty games. The district playoffs were next, and what the *Pioneer* had dubbed "the Drive for Five" state titles was on for real.

On top of the stands, Jay Overmiller and Greg Hobelmann held their hands aloft and waited for Christian and Robbie to lower the television gear by rope from the wooden press box. It was the only way they could get it out. Gavin slumped on a bench nearby. His cold had worsened, and he wanted to ride home in the truck with his father instead of on the team bus.

It was late, and it would be after one in the morning before anyone got back home, but Jay and Greg were in a good mood.

"Well?" asked Greg.

Jay scooped up a half-asleep Gavin.

"The season ain't half over," Jay said. "It's just beginning."

They both smiled.

# 12

This is the start of your chapter, the beginning of how you're going to be remembered in Redmen football history.

—Roger Barta, October 13, 2008

Kris Lehmann and Colt Rogers stopped by Coach Barta's office to talk about a proper punishment for forgetting to bring their jerseys to the Colby game. They suggested some extra running before or after practice for perhaps as long as a week. Coach Barta said he would think about it. He could tell that Kris and Colt had taken their mistake seriously and were sorry. Maybe that was enough. Maybe he was mellowing.

It was a sunny October afternoon, and his team was on the practice field attacking the blocking sled one after another, chanting "hit, hit, hit" as they moved it down the practice field with Brock Hutchinson on board in his best George Washington pose. Laughter came from the back of the lines, signaling the Redmen had wind and were in shape and relaxed.

Coach Barta knew they had come through the toughest stretch of the season better than they had started. With the exception of Trenton Terrill, they were relatively healthy.

They were beaten up a bit, but the Redmen had three weeks for their aches and pains to heal, and for their minds to clear to refocus. The route to a state title was long and littered with titles: a district and bi-district championship, as well as regional, sectional, and substate games. The only one that mattered around here was seven games away at Fort Hays State and was for the state championship.

From here on in, the Redmen were only playing schools in their classification, 2A, and Coach Barta knew their first two opponents were overmatched. Washington County, Friday's opponent, only had twenty-two players and had two victories against four losses, and the following week, the Redmen played 3–4 Osborne. Then they had a bye week.

Coach Barta called his team together. He was feeling feisty and philosophical. "We pretty healthy, guys?" he asked.

There were head nods. Nobody disagreed.

"Marshall?" Coach Barta asked.

Against Colby, Marshall had gotten his breath taken away when he caught a hard hit to the groin.

"I'm fine," Marshall said.

"Someday you're going to learn what those are for," he said. Marshall turned crimson as the team roared.

"You have worked hard and improved every day, and that's what life is all about," Coach Barta said. "I'm sure you get tired of me saying that. But when I'm in the graveyard, I'll still be haunting you with that thought every day.

"You know I like practice a whole lot better than I like games," he said. "Don't I, Coach Hutch?"

"We all do, Coach," Big Hutch replied. "It's where the real teaching gets done. It's where we get to know you boys and pass on our wisdom."

"That's right," Coach Barta said. "I think this time of

year is the most fun part of the season. I got to tell you, though, I also get a little bit sad around now."

The coach paused and looked around at his team.

"See, guys, I know that this time of year, we're running out of practices. Theoretically, we can have maybe only a week or so left, to be together like this. So let's work hard together and enjoy each other every day now.

"I don't want this to end, do you, guys?" Coach Barta asked.

"No, sir," came their firm reply.

"Every game from here on out is for a championship," he said. "This is the start of your chapter, the beginning of how you're going to be remembered in Redmen football history."

"Yes, sir," the Redmen said.

"All right, passing drills," he said.

With that, the Redmen scattered for thirty-five minutes of pass plays and formations, most of which they would never use in a game. I sometimes thought Coach Barta put his team through the elaborate passing drills so he could catch up with the visitors on the practice sidelines. He barely watched Travis and Ethan and Shawn Stansbury and Alex Hobelmann work on their throwing. In fact, so far this season, Smith Center had put the ball in the air only a half-dozen times.

When I asked Coach Barta how many pass plays were in the Smith Center playbook, he was succinct.

"A lot more than I need," he said.

This brought a chuckle from Morse Boucher, who was planted among the cluster of coaches. He was here almost every day this time of year, not wanting to miss a minute of the Redmen's championship drive.

"I go to coaching clinics about passing all the time, but I guess I don't know much how to teach it," Coach Barta said.

Behind him, the quarterbacks took turns winging the ball to receivers, who began routes from spread formations. As soon as he flung a long pass, Travis Rempe skipped down the field with his arms up in the touchdown signal and adopted the baritone of a television announcer.

"Rempe just hit Osburn with a perfect strike at the 40-yard line, 35-, 30-, 20-, Osburn . . . will . . . go . . . all . . . the WAYYYY!"

He might have been an eight-year-old playing in his backyard. Coach Barta smiled at his quarterback's fantasy.

"I think football is an easy game, and I try to make it that way," said Coach Barta. "It's about blocking and tackling. I watch the colleges and see how they run that spread offense. They got a couple of things I don't have. One is a ton of talent. The other is the stomach to throw it all the time."

"You got tough kids, Coach," Morse said.

Coach Barta smiled.

"Yes, I do," he said.

———

Washington County was the last scheduled home game, which meant it was parents' night. Before the game, each senior and his parents were introduced and promenaded before the stands. Each mom clutched a rose and her son's arm. Each dad squeezed into his boy's away jersey.

It was an important night to Coach Barta, and he wanted it to be important to his team. He told the Redmen to go home and hug their parents tonight, and every night.

"Things happen, guys," he told them. "We don't live forever. Someday, guys, they're going to be in a hospital bed dying, and your hearts are going to be breaking. You're going to want them to know how much you love them."

As they made their way onto the track, it was hard to tell who was prouder, the boys or their folks. The applause was thunderous and sustained. The seniors had earned the town's admiration. No one argued that they were as talented as last year's bunch. They had looked mortal, or worse, earlier in the season and probably should have lost at Norton. But they never got down on themselves. And they never quit.

Justin Nixon was walking on air with a full-blown smile as he escorted his parents, Joe and Marsha. Trenton Terrill hobbled on his knee brace in between Amy and John. The Rempes neatly solved the dilemma of having twins on the team: Bill wore Travis's no. 9 jersey, and Stacy wore Trevor's no. 8. Marshall McCall stood between Shane and Susan, and all three pairs of eyes were glistening with tears. The Maces, the Tuckers, the Lehmanns, the Easteses, the Duntzses, the Troys, and the other Nixons followed.

Even though they were young men, they looked like boys, especially when the ceremony was closing, and they hugged their mothers and exchanged those awkward handshakes and half hugs with their fathers.

It did not take the Redmen long to reconvene with their parents in the locker room. They crushed Washington County, 68–0. The junior varsity played the second half, and the clock remained running. Early in the fourth quarter, "61" rose in the sky, shining on the wheat field, lighting up the tractors. Only six more victories stood between the Redmen and the state record of sixty-seven victories.

After the game, the locker room was more packed than

usual because it was the one home game when mothers were allowed in for the circle-up. Coach Barta stared in the corner at Kalen Mace, whose normally stone-faced demeanor was cracked by an ear-to-ear grin. Kalen's father, Dave, had played for Coach Barta, and Kalen's mother, Lynae, now looked about as ecstatic as her son.

Coach Barta had actually called a pass play in this game, and Travis delivered the ball to Kalen for an eleven-yard gain. It was the first catch of Kalen's varsity career.

"I don't know who was more surprised the ball was in the air coming your way," Coach Barta said. "You or your mom."

He let the laughter subside.

"I really just want to thank every mom and dad in here for what you do for me and my coaches and this program," he said. "We would not have the success without your support. And I really want to thank you for these young men. They have shown that they are a special group. I'm grateful I get to spend the time I do with them."

After the prayer, the players took a seat on the stools in front of their lockers. There was no rush to shower with their mothers in the room. This also was the one time of the year they were allowed to join their husbands and the rest of the men in town in walking all four walls of the locker room to shake every player's hand. The ritual took longer than usual.

No one complained.

Roger and Pam Barta had invited people over to their house, something they used to do after every game, but after thirty years of coaching and forty-one years of marriage, it was now a once-a-season event.

After twenty-eight years at the bank, Pam was the new director of Smith County Economic Development, a job badly in need of her whirlwind energy. Coach Barta had warned me about Pam as soon as I got to town.

"You just got to learn to say no to her, or she'll have you running all around," he said.

It was impossible to deny Pam Barta, and the number of projects she kept going all at once was evidence of it. Her plate was full creating a job succession program, which matched existing businesses with aging owners to younger folks for on-the-job training. She was trying to reclaim abandoned buildings for the town, and to attract new businesses to fill them. There was the world-class bird hunting to pitch to travel agencies. There were windmill companies to lure and young people to persuade to return home. Pam had already secured Smith Center's first bus, and bus service, and now she was pushing for a preschool.

She also knew her football—how could she not after forty-one years of Friday night football? At home games, however, she barely was able to watch because of the blizzard of business conversations and everyday small-town catching up. She preferred listening to Tad Felts's broadcast of the away games and confessed that, for the first time in years, she had paced anxiously around her family room throughout the Norton game.

The Bartas lived in a gracious home off Main Street, where they had raised their three children, Brooks, Shelby, and Carrie—all of whom had kids of their own now and were living away from Smith Center. Brooks and Carrie were in Kansas, while Shelby was in Phoenix, Arizona. Even so, the Barta house remained kid-friendly, with toys and sawed-off furniture for their eight grandchildren, who ranged in age from four months to ten years.

The Bartas had old and close friends in town who gathered for the postgame celebration. Ken Depperschmidt, the coach's fraternity brother at college, who had recommended him for this job thirty years ago, was here. He was an insurance agent and a member of the Redmen's statistics crew, whose members, like the crew who worked the sideline chains, had been friends of the Bartas and stalwarts of the Smith Center sideline for decades. Many of them were there for chili and navy bean soup and some beers. As were Big and Little Hutch, Mike Rogers, and Tim Wilson.

Before Coach Barta could join the party, however, he had to accept one phone call and make another one. Cullen Riner, the Osborne coach, was on the phone to arrange where and when they would exchange game film Saturday morning. It was a weekly rite for high school coaches in western Kansas to meet each other between their two towns to exchange film. Sometimes, they had coffee. Other times, they met on the side of the road. Always, they spent some time either lamenting how bad their team was, or playing down how good they were. Osborne was only twenty-four miles away, but Riner was traveling on Saturday and wanted to make the exchange at six thirty in the morning.

It was awfully early for a confirmed sleeper like Coach Barta, but he agreed to it, and then took the phone into the garage to call his son. Brooks Barta had followed his father into teaching math and coaching high school football and, according to Roger, was better than him in both. In twelve seasons, Brooks had already won more than one hundred games at Holton High School and two 4A state titles. He ran the same offense and adhered to the same principles he had learned from his father.

Coach Barta had loved coaching his son at Smith Center, and they both claimed that they never brought problems from the football field home. When Brooks earned a scholarship to play for Kansas State, Coach Barta and Pam spent four years driving to every one of his games, which often meant leaving late Friday night after coaching the Redmen and driving overnight.

Whenever the media and the fans agitated for the two schools to play each other, Brooks and Coach Barta had the same response: "Momma won't like it."

So each Friday night, they called each other to compare notes on their games, or cheer each other up when necessary, though these days it was rarely required. Brooks's Wildcats had defeated Atchison earlier in the night, so father and son were each in very good spirits. One thing Coach Barta fretted over in regard to Brooks was the road not taken. He got wistful about the choices he had made over his long tenure here in Smith Center.

Bigger schools had come calling, and he once very nearly went to Emporia. He withdrew from consideration after he and Pam decided it was unfair to pull Shelby out of the high school. In 2003, with everyone grown up, he pursued the job at Washburn Rural in Topeka, which was in Class 6A, the state's largest classification.

He did not get the job because, he heard, of his age.

"I wonder what it would have been like to coach at a big high school or even in college," he told me. "You can't help it. I'd like to know how I would have stacked up against the best.

"I know Brooks is a better coach than me," he said. "He had some opportunities to coach at colleges, but he turned them down because he knew he would not have had much of a home life with his wife and kids. Hell, you can't live your kids' life for them. You can only love them."

# PART FOUR

# CIRCLE UP

# 13

The games you play in November are the ones you remember.

— Roger Barta, November 2, 2008

It was Thursday, the night before Halloween, and the Redmen were wearing their game jerseys as they stood near the sideline in Phillipsburg, watching the Panthers play Beloit in a 3A district game. The Redmen were off this week and awaiting their playoff assignment after dusting off the Osborne Bulldogs, 60–0, the previous week. The Redmen's fourth straight shutout had been as perfect a game as you could ask for to launch a playoff run. Their offense was in playoff gear, too, having put 208 points on the board over the four shutouts.

Against the Bulldogs, the Redmen ran for a season-high 611 yards, and Joe Osburn turned in a breakout performance. He scored four touchdowns on runs of sixty-three, forty-five, sixty-three, and seventy-one yards. He was a one-man highlight film as he ran past and over Bulldogs, as well as spinning away from and cutting through them. Joe could not have turned it on at a more opportune time. There were coaches from Hutchinson and Butler junior colleges in the stands, as well as coaches from the four-year Sterling College, where another former Redman, Andy Lambert, now coached. He had given scholarships to five of last year's seniors, and a couple of them had come to watch as well.

Joe was radiant as he accepted congratulations. His smile was as blinding as a lighthouse for the first time all season.

But the Redmen had played the game with a heavy heart. The day before, Steve Kloster, the town chiropractor, had died while on his morning jog. His death had knocked the whole town on its heels; Steve was vigorous at age fifty-six, ate healthy, and exercised regularly. Seven weeks ago, Mary and I were in his home, eating soup and listening to what made Smith Center special.

What most did not know was that five years earlier, Steve had been diagnosed with a heart condition: the muscle wall was thickening. There was no medication to put him on, but doctors told him that if he ever developed a spasmodic heartbeat he would die instantly. That, apparently, was what had occurred.

"I think he put one foot down on the street in Smith Center, Kansas, and the next foot came down in heaven as he was being ushered to the throne of Jesus," his wife, Janet, told the *Smith County Pioneer*.

His passing had hit the Redmen hard. Marshall, Kris, Travis, Trevor, and Colt—all wrestlers—took a ball signed by the whole team over to Janet at her home. All of them dissolved into tears. They were no less devastated the following Monday, as they helped to serve the lunch after Steve was laid to rest. In his death, he had given the boys much to think about. They saw photographs of him as a young man with long hair and atop a motorcycle, which was hard to reconcile with the mild-mannered, neatly trimmed chiropractor who was a board member of the Evangelical Free Church. The final words Steve left also indicated that he had given great thought to his spiritual journey.

"I have just fully begun to understand my role as a father and spouse," he had written. "I tried to be a good role model and spiritual head for my family. I have fallen short in many areas. Sometimes I got my priorities too high and put my family too high or too low.

"I feel fortunate to have had Janet as a wonderful wife, often giving me more respect and honor than I deserved. My kids have been raised in the nature of the Lord as best as we could. I was lost for many years and I didn't even know it. I have changed for the better since I accepted Jesus Christ as my savior."

Coach Barta knew that the week had been emotional for his team, so he kept the practices short and focused. He knew the boys wanted to go watch Phillipsburg tonight, so they only stretched and ran without pads before Coach Barta sent them home at five in the afternoon. He actually wished that he could go with them. Instead, he and the staff were fanning out across Kansas to scout possible playoff opponents. He and Mike Rogers were on their way to Wa-Keeney to watch Trego, the Redmen's likely first-round foe.

Little Hutch was going to Salina to see Sacred Heart, a team they might see in the second round. Big Hutch was easing his Cadillac Coupe de Ville three hours south to La Crosse to see the best game of the evening: La Crosse versus Meade. Both were unbeaten, and La Crosse had perhaps the best player in the state in Marshall Musil, the six-foot-two, 220-pound running back who had already verbally accepted a scholarship from the University of Oklahoma.

I had chosen to go to Phillipsburg for burgers and the

game with Shane McCall, John Terrill, and Dave Mace—the fathers of Marshall, Trenton, and Kalen. They all worked at the People's Bank and were close friends. I climbed into the jump seat of Shane's truck with John and his youngest son, Kale, who, because he was a freshman, was bounced from his brothers' ride in favor of an upperclassman. I was immediately given a slip of paper and told to predict how many combined points would be put on the board in the first quarter, first half, and final score as well who would win the game, and commanded to ante up a dollar.

Over hamburgers and a couple of pitchers of beer at a tavern near the stadium, they told me about their recent trip with their sons to Colorado to watch Kansas State play. For years now, each fall they had taken their boys to a Wildcats road game. They usually left after the Redmen's game Friday night and drove through the night to Missouri, Texas, Oklahoma, and now Colorado. It was a bonding trip.

John had Kale and Dave had Brandon, both of whom were freshmen, which ensured that the tradition would carry on a few more years. Shane was more melancholy. He hoped he might be able to persuade Marshall to continue the tradition in college, but knew that he could not count on it, especially if his son decided to pursue his dream of playing football. Marshall had already been accepted academically at Kansas, K-State, and Fort Hays, and Shane was trying to persuade him to choose one of those and go be a student.

Shane was also worried about his son's health. The concussion Marshall had suffered in the opening game had scared him. He had endured the toll college football takes on a body. He knew that after a first concussion the likelihood increases of suffering another one. Marshall, though, had his heart set on playing football in college somewhere. He argued to his mom and dad that they had played sports in college and remained healthy and successful in the classroom.

Sterling, Bethany, and other small colleges in the Kansas Collegiate Athletic Conference were interested in having Marshall play football for them. Marshall, however, was more interested in the junior colleges like Butler and Hutchinson. Both schools played in the Jayhawk Conference, which was ultracompetitive and often a way station for Division I talents who needed to raise their grades.

The league was legendary for sending football players into four-year colleges and on to the pros. Running back Rudi Johnson, for example, went from Butler to Auburn University and then to the Cincinnati Bengals and the Detroit Lions. Marshall was a realist; he knew he was never going to make it to the National Football League. But he was earnest and did not want to commit to a four-year school and then possibly disappoint a coach if he decided that he did not want to play football in college. At a junior college, Marshall felt he could discover how passionate he was about football, test himself against top competition, and then perhaps earn a football scholarship to a four-year-school.

The more they talked, the more it was clear how much Shane, John, and Dave enjoyed watching their boys go through the Redmen football program. They were sad as well that it was nearing its end. They talked about returning to officiating high school games, a hobby they gave up with no regrets when their boys entered high school. Shane and Dave kept statistics and prowled the sidelines, far more nervous than Marshall and Kalen seemed to be. Shane, especially, writhed and twisted when teams tried to pass on Marshall. Shane was a former defensive back, after all, and would grimace if his son turned the wrong way. John was the voice of the Redmen, and he and Don Wick had taken to wearing wireless headsets on the sidelines instead of sitting up in the press box. They had the best seats in the house.

We paid our check, walked across a parking lot into the Phillipsburg Stadium, and lo and behold about half of Smith Center was there. Most of them had gone over to the visitor's side or were standing on the fence that separated the grandstands. The Redmen were gathered near the south end zone on the Beloit side as well. Justin Nixon was working his way through a foot-long meatball sandwich from the nearby Subway. It looked like a hot dog in his massive hand. Marshall, Colt, Kalen, Trenton, Travis, Trevor—just about the whole team was there. They were rooting for Phillipsburg, which was 4–4, against undefeated Beloit.

When the Panthers withstood a late Beloit charge to upset the Trojans, 13–12, the Redmen went onto the field to congratulate them like old friends, which in many instances they were.

We had just left Phillipsburg's city limits when Shane's cell phone rang. It was Marshall. He was turning eighteen the following day and was looking to start the celebration early.

"There's school tomorrow, and I want you home by 10:30 p.m.," Shane said. "I mean it. You guys don't need to be cruising around Phillipsburg. You drive slow, too. You don't need to get a ticket in Phillips County."

There was pause, as Shane listened to his son.

"Hey, Marsh," he said. "I love you."

---

Darren Sasse staggered into the NASA Lab under the weight of a three-foot-high stack of scouting reports. He dropped them on a desk, and they landed with a thud.

"There's a guy in Brazil telling his crew to start up their chainsaws and clear-cut those five thousand acres: Smith Center is in the playoffs again," he said, bringing a belly laugh from Coach Barta.

This was the time of the season that really mattered for the Redmen, and to underscore that point the very first sentence of the scouting report for their opening-round opponent said, "The games you play in November are the ones you remember."

It was going to be a hectic week for the Redmen. They would play Trego at home in two days, on Tuesday, which was election night. Then, presumably, they would host a second-round game on Saturday. Trego was 4–5, and the Golden Eagles' coach, Myron Flax, told Coach Barta that his team had not improved since holding the Redmen to eight points in the first half of the second game of the season and probably did not have a prayer against them now. No one in the NASA Lab here today disagreed with him.

After comparing notes on the games each had scouted and calling their coaching buddies around the state for reconnaissance, Coach Barta had a pretty good idea of who the Redmen might face in the next five games, and they all expected to play all the way to the title game. Their team was not the same tentative and fumble-prone bunch that had stumbled through the first four games. They had not allowed a team to score in four games, averaging 450 yards rushing and fifty-two points a game over that span.

What was fascinating was how Coach Barta had started to deploy more of his offensive weapons and integrate his younger players into the team's playing rotation. He was like a pool player, sinking one shot while carefully setting up the next.

Early in the season, Colt and Trevor got the bulk of the carries. The Redmen offense was essentially pound, pound, pound the middle with Trevor and then let Colt follow Justin off tackle and into the end zone. Over the past four games Coach Barta was letting Travis keep the ball more and scamper around the ends, as well as attempting a pass now and then. He was calling Joe Osburn's number more often and letting him zip through the right side of the line behind Cody Tucker and Kalen Mace. Marshall was getting the ball more on offense, too. He did not have Colt's vision and slipperiness, nor was he as fast as Joe, but he was more powerful and punishing than either of them. No one could arm tackle him, and once Marshall picked up steam he could run over or past defensive players.

It was a tactical decision to turn the talented Redmen loose gradually over time. Coach Barta wanted opposing coaches to puzzle over his team, to worry about things they had not yet seen on film as well as what they already had. Every coach in the state knew Smith Center was going to put seven linemen shoulder to shoulder and run the ball down their throats, but they were never exactly sure who was going to get the ball or which direction he was going to take it.

Coach Barta also was increasing the playing time of his sophomores and juniors, seasoning them for next year. Shawn Stansbury was getting meaningful snaps in the secondary, and Matt Atwood, a rock of a junior, was staking claim to one of the defensive end positions. The sophomore McNary twins, Aaron and Dereck, were being plugged in the secondary during the first halves of games and appearing on offense in the backfield before it was cleanup time with the varsity line.

"There are a lot of reasons he's a great coach," Brock Hutchinson told me, "but one of the most important is how he can look five games or even a season away and figure out what kid he's going to need then, and how he is going to get him there. You go back over his career and you'll see by the playoffs each year, we have thirty-five to forty guys who have developed. They would be starters on most teams."

Another virtue that made Roger Barta a great coach was that he respected his boys and their intelligence. He was a tremendous motivator, but one who believed that the best way to get his team's juices flowing was to be honest and show faith in them. After scouting the opposition and breaking down game film, he and his staff had decided that the Redmen would easily win their first two playoff games. So there was no sense in telling the Redmen otherwise. Kids knew when you did not believe your own fire and brimstone. Instead, Coach Barta told his coaches that the theme for the next week would be for the Redmen to challenge each other in practice so they would be worthy of the rewards that lay ahead.

"Good on good, Coach," said Tim Wilson.

It was yet another Redman mantra uttered at most practices, and one that was a rallying call for the Black Shirts to push the starters as hard as they could. It was mostly a painful task that involved emulating that week's opponents' offense and defense. More often than not, the Black Shirts were learning them on the fly, and so they got absolutely pounded by the first team. Tim was the coach of the Black Shirts at practice, calling their plays from a binder that he held aloft so everyone could see.

He was their patron saint as well. He winced when they got creamed and encouraged them when they got the better of the starters. He paid attention. When a Black Shirt limped back to the huddle and looked as if he wanted to be anywhere but there, Tim always seemed to have the right words to lift his spirits.

"You're one of our smartest players," he told Kaden Roush one day after the sophomore was sandwiched by Kris Lehmann and Joel Osburn with a hit that took even my breath away. "You were right on top of that run. Now you get up after a hit like that, and it makes me think you're one of our toughest players."

Suddenly, Kaden had his wind back and was lining up for more. So "good on good" would be the mantra for the next five games over a compact five weeks.

———

After the game with Trego on Tuesday, it was likely that Sacred Heart would be coming to Hubbard Stadium on Saturday. The Knights were a Catholic school from Salina who threw the ball a lot.

"They are 6–4 and don't play any defense," said Brock. "They got a pretty good quarterback. He can wing it, and he's a tough kid. Still, we're a lot better than them."

But it was the third playoff game, a week from Friday, that the Redmen coaches could not wait to play. It was the game they were certain would yield the eventual state champion—either the Redmen, the La Crosse Leopards, or the St. Francis Indians.

Big Hutch had been impressed as he watched La Crosse dismantle previously undefeated Meade, 51–7, on October 30.

"They're the real deal," he said. "They got athletes. The line is beefy and disciplined. Their quarterback, this Jeremy Garcia, is cocky, quick, and likes to score. They have speed outside, and Marshall Musil is everything that they say he is. He is big, smart, and tough. I don't imagine Bob Stoops over there in Oklahoma makes too many mistakes on kids.

"It should be a helluva game," he predicted.

"I want anyone but Tim," Coach Barta said.

Everyone picked up the reference to Tim Lambert, the coach of St. Francis. Tim was the younger brother of Andy Lambert, the coach at Sterling College, and another Smith Center product. He was a former quarterback for Coach Barta and the Redmen, and also the cousin of Mike Rogers's wife, Cally. Tim Lambert had built a powerhouse program over sixteen years at St. Francis by basically becoming Smith Center West. The Indians ran the same offense, put a premium on hitting, and preached the character-building gospel. The problem was that for the past four years St. Francis had been on a collision course with the Redmen in the playoffs. They were a difficult matchup on the field because each team knew the other's plays and philosophies. In the 2006 substate championship, the Indians lost to the Redmen 6–2, the lowest-scoring game in the Smith Center streak and one that was said to be like watching two bulldozers bang into each other for forty-eight minutes.

It was a more difficult matchup emotionally as well. The two coaches were close, and as much as Coach Barta disliked having to beat one of his protégés, the thought of losing to one wasn't much better. "It's no fun playing him," Coach Barta said. "Plus, he's due to beat us."

The Redmen were getting only one day of "good on good" before the playoff opener with Trego. Brock, Mike, and Tim put them through a brisk practice on Monday as Coach Barta and Big Hutch wandered the practice fields.

Throughout the fall, Coach Barta and Big Hutch had been tuned in to the presidential election and the worsening financial crisis. Their retirement pensions were tied up in the market and taking a beating. They were especially interested in the presidential election and sensed the senator from Illinois, Barack Obama, was going to become the first African American president. They were planning to vote for him, along with the rest of the coaching staff, and many of the educators in the school district.

"It's been a fun year," Big Hutch said to no one in particular.

"We've had to work a lot more than we have had to recently," offered Coach Barta. "That's what's made it fun."

Coach Barta then headed off toward Tim and the offense.

"I told Coach Barta that I'd stay as long as he did," Big Hutch told me. "I don't think I'll ever not have fun here."

The team was subdued at the end of practice, and the coaches did not offer any inspirational pyrotechnics to raise their pulses. This was a relaxed and confident group.

"We got an election tomorrow, and I know some of you are eighteen and have the opportunity to vote for the first time," Coach Barta said. "We are the greatest country in the world, and we live in one of the greatest towns in this country. Be proud of that, and make sure you vote."

There were no surprises on Election Day in Smith Center, Kansas. The Redmen pounded Trego, and the John McCain–Sarah Palin ticket swept Smith County and the rest of Kansas. The *Pioneer* went to press on Tuesday night, so there was no real analysis in the newspaper of either Barack Obama's historic victory or the overpowering first step the Redmen took toward tying the state record of five straight titles, or setting a new record with sixty-seven consecutive victories.

Instead, there was an eight-by-eleven-inch insert under the *Smith County Pioneer* logo. Since all politics is local, results from the county races took up the first two columns, and the results from the U.S. House and Senate races filled the third column. The fourth column led off with McCain-Palin with 1,695 votes, and Obama-Biden with 437—a 75 percent to 25 percent split that mirrored the results of a mock election held in the high school earlier in the day.

And since the Redmen bridged all differences in Smith County, the two-column-by-four-inch shaded box with a bold typeface in the bottom-right-hand quarter of the page told the real story why November is important in Smith Center.

SMITH CENTER vs. TREGO
Tuesday, Nov. 4, 2008

GAME SCORE
Smith Center.....62
Trego..............0

Regional Game at Hubbard Field
Saturday, Nov. 8—7 P.M.

# 14

I mean tackle them really hard. I mean hit like Smith Center hits people.

—Ivan Burgess, November 14, 2008

They rolled into the Pizza Hut like locusts, grabbing their pies, chicken wings, pasta, and cinnamon twists off steel racks without breaking stride. It was the night before the playoff game against Sacred Heart, and the Redmen were having their team meal as they did on the eve of every game. Leo Tuxhorn had gathered their orders before practice and dropped them off to Mary VanderGeisen, who in turn cranked up the pizza-making enterprise. Some brought their own bottles of Mountain Dew; most kept the waitresses, Chelsea McDonald and Shelby Johnson, in constant motion dropping off Pepsis and iced teas. Chelsea was a senior and Shelby a junior, and they unflappably fielded their classmates' requests.

Most of the town knew that if you wanted pizza the night before a game, it was best to wait until after seven o'clock, when the boys cleared out. Still, there always seemed to be a traveler or two whose eyes widened as the Redmen swept through in their green-and-red letter jackets. The noise level went up several decibels as boxes of pizzas were passed in the air from one corner of the tiny dining room to the other. Who sat where appeared to be haphazard, but there was definitely a hierarchy in place. Justin and Josh Nixon commanded the booth by the bathrooms, and the other linemen were clustered at booths and tables around them. This was where most of the pizza boxes were being passed, and some prodigious eating was under way.

The seniors who were not linemen—Marshall, Trevor, Travis, Trenton, Joe, Joel, Kalen, and Ethan—also were assured booths along the walls. The freshmen and sophomores were left at the tables in the center of the room or standing up until they could squeeze into a booth or steal a chair.

Justin had kept his word to not shave all season. His beard was getting pretty scruffy; it looked like steel wool that was coming apart after scouring too many iron skillets. He had been invited back to Kansas State the following Saturday for the Nebraska game, and he thought he would trim it before his trip. He was having a good year, and colleges were noticing. He was an immovable force on both sides of the ball, and the weight loss had added extra steps to his quickness. I got a glimpse of what opposing players were up against when Justin came barreling off the field at the Trego game. Big Hutch had sent in a late substitution for him, and Justin had to get off the field before the Golden Eagles snapped the ball or accept a penalty.

I had been looking somewhere else when I heard a commotion on the sideline and turned to see Justin rumbling off the field, picking up momentum like a boulder rolling down a mountain. The underclassmen had already made way, and it was Kale Terrill, Trenton's little brother, who mercifully grabbed me by the collar and yanked me aside an instant before Big Nix pancaked me. I was grateful.

Justin also was in the best shape of his Smith Center career. He had played both offensive and defensive tackle most games with only a few snaps off for rest. He was far tougher in practice as well, answering the bell for every drill.

At home he had a box full of letters from virtually every junior college and small college in Kansas, Missouri, and Nebraska. Kansas State had been very interested in him, but the Wildcats' coach, Ron Prince, had been fired two days earlier and a replacement had not been named. Justin was worried, rightly so, that he might get lost in the transition between coaching staffs. He was disappointed as well that he would have to sell himself all over again. Still, he was going to see the Wildcats play against Nebraska next week and tell the K-State coaches that he was ready to play.

The recruiting process had been good for Justin's self-esteem. He had redoubled his efforts to learn how to organize his time to study, and he was talking as if college was not only a possibility but also perhaps something he really, really wanted. Justin was clearly most comfortable with his old teammates now playing at Sterling College. They had kept in touch and made sure to seek him out on the field after the Osborne game. Unfortunately, Sterling was not in the NCAA, but in the NAIA, which did not offer full athletic scholarships. Instead, these schools tried to put together a mixture of financial aid and academic scholarship. Justin was not sure if Sterling, or any other small college, would be able to offer a package that he and his family could afford.

The rest of the seniors were going to have to decide if they really wanted to play football in college. Trenton Terrill aspired to be a doctor and could go where he wanted. In addition to his football talents, he was a good enough baseball player to attract some interest from area schools. He was shopping for a college that offered a recognized premed program, where he could also play baseball. Kalen Mace understood that this was the end of football for him as well; he wanted to go to Kansas State. Trevor and Travis Rempe were counting down their football careers, too. Trevor wanted to go to vocational school in Manhattan, Kansas, and become a linesman like his father. Travis wanted to join the Air Force National Guard and continue school in another year or two. Kris Lehmann and Joe and Joel Osburn wanted to keep playing and were looking at Sterling or Tabor College as well as junior colleges.

Now, however, they were unified by the thought of finishing the season undefeated, winning another state title, and being the team that set the record for the most consecutive victories in the state.

The Redmen rolled out of Pizza Hut with the same fury they had rolled in, hopped in their pickups and cars, and moved their unity-building evening two and half minutes away to Marshall's shed. One Redman after another came through the doorway with more Pizza Hut boxes. As I watched the riot over who got to play Ping-Pong first and listened to the laughter accompanying the wrestling match for the Xbox, I understood how a team that had started the season playing not to lose had been transformed into one that believed its destiny was to win.

All these Redmen needed was to learn to respect and like each other, just as Coach Barta had told them on the first day of practice, before they could realize their potential. The respect quotient had been filled at Norton, when they survived their own mistakes and the bigger and perhaps harder-hitting

Bluejays. They had not turned against each other for their many mistakes. They had not quit. They stopped Norton's two-point conversion and had gotten out of town with a victory. It was the spark of a revelation that the seniors were just now coming to understand.

"It was a rough one," Marshall said of the near-humiliation at Norton. "But I think it opened our eyes to how much work was needed."

Marshall was not oblivious to the commotion going on in his clubhouse. He watched it unfold with a smile. He was proud of it. The Redmen were loose. Ready. They were a team, and Marshall, at least, understood why. They loved each other. Finally.

"Looking back now, we weren't very good," he said. "But we definitely stuck it out when we had to. We just weren't fitting together yet. We were trying to make plays, but they were plays for one person. We hadn't grasped the team aspect, I don't think."

It had been the first significant step in a journey that now had four games left before it was finished. They had worked together through fifty-five practices and nine games, and they were fresher now than when they started. They really didn't need any extra motivation, but the Sacred Heart quarterback, Conner Martin, had told one of the newspapers that the Knights wanted to play the Redmen. "Let them hit us with their best shot. No offense to Pat Benatar or anything," he said, paraphrasing the title of the song that the singer that made a hit in 1980.

The quote found its way onto the Redmen's locker room bulletin board, and the song onto the Smith Center sound system before the game.

"Who's Pat Benatar?" I heard Travis ask Trevor, quite

justifiably, since neither of them was born when the song was on the charts.

Before the game, Brock Hutchinson decided to have some fun at the Sacred Heart quarterback's expense. He knew the Knights would try to throw thirty or forty times, so he installed a series of stunts for his offensive linemen, and blitzes for his linebackers, to harass Martin.

"When you hit him," he said, "and you will hit him, then I want you to give him a hand up and ask him—nicely, of course—if you can borrow his Pat Benatar tape. Or you can just say, 'I'll be right back.' Or, 'Tell your coach to run the ball; otherwise you're going to get hit.'"

It turned out to be the kind of night typical of Kansas in the winter, but one I had yet to encounter. The twenty-five-mile-per-hour winds were swirling the cold and the rain and made Hubbard Stadium feel like the bottom of a snow-cone machine. It was a passing team's nightmare, and Martin and the Knights had to endure it. Dillon Corbett, Logan Tuxhorn, Kris Lehmann, and Trevor Rempe sacked the Sacred Heart quarterback. Joe Osburn intercepted him, as did Marshall, who was quietly becoming the Redmen's most fearsome defender. Martin and the Knights did not get anywhere near the end zone on their first seven possessions.

The Redmen, meanwhile, were unstoppable, and Coach Barta allowed every one of his offensive threats a chance to command the spotlight—or at least an intimidating piece of game film for the coaching staff of next week's playoff opponent to chew on. The Redmen scored on their first eleven possessions, and seven of the first eight possessions lasted four plays or less. Colt, Joe, Marshall, Travis, and Trevor combined for 456 yards and seven touchdowns—all before halftime, when the Redmen led, 56–0. Colt had three of the scores and 260 yards, and did not carry the ball in the second half. Marshall powered for two touchdowns and 103 yards. In the second half, playing with the junior varsity, Dereck McNary ran for 67 yards and another score.

On the opening play of the fourth quarter, with the score 67–7, Coach Barta let Logan Tuxhorn attempt his first field goal of the season, a twenty-seven-yarder. Even that went through. The final score was emphatic: Smith Center 73, Sacred Heart 20. As the team gathered at midfield to accept and get their picture taken with the plaque they had now earned as regional champions, Mike Hughes, the Redmen's public address announcer, broke into the celebration.

"We have a final—La Crosse 38, St. Francis 30," he said.

"Good, that's who we wanted," said Marshall.

"Bring on Marshall Musil," said Trevor.

"I guess we'll see what a Division I player looks like," said Logan Tuxhorn, smiling.

———

Mary, Jack, and I were out at the Roush place the following day to visit our first hog farm and to have Sunday dinner with Jesse, Kaden, and their mother, Sue. Their father, Kelly Roush, was taking advantage of a relatively dry day and was out on the combine bringing in the milo. Like everyone else around here, he was behind with the harvest.

Just as the Tuckers were my professors of cattle, and the Overmillers taught me Farming 101, the Roushes were my guides to hog farming. Jesse and Kaden had bought out their parents' interest in the family hog operation and now tended forty-five sows and some seven hundred hogs. They showed the best ones and sold the others, and together Jesse and Kaden were rightfully proud of their enterprise. Jesse, a junior, was the older of the two and logged a lot of time at defensive end, often as a starter. Kaden was a sophomore, learning his way through the Redmen system and playing junior varsity.

They were different personalities with different passions and aspirations. Both were excellent students and thoughtful young men. Jesse, however, was the quieter of the two, and the one who savored football more. He worked hard on the Roushes' 2,300 acres, but he did not particularly like the lifestyle. He did not want to come back here to farm, and instead was hoping to go to Kansas State and study agricultural engineering in the hope of designing farm machinery.

"I like the aggression of football," he said. "I like the release from the quiet and hard work of farming."

Kaden, on the other hand, preferred farming to football. He intended to come home after college and remain in the family business. He also was anything but quiet. Kaden was gregarious and articulate with the communication gifts of a politician. He had recently captured the top prize in a job interview contest sponsored by the Future Farmers of America, and a couple of weeks earlier had taken some time off from football to attend the FFA's national convention in Indianapolis. There, he took third place in a science competition for the ethanol distiller that he had built. He loved his hogs as well, tending to them with nutritional oversight and tender loving care for the many shows in which he entered them.

Sue Roush was a force of nature herself, with a loud and exuberant laugh that warmed a room. She immediately took Mary, Jack, and me to the mud room off to the side of her home, which was built in 1906, and gave us some hooded sweatshirts and muck boots.

"You don't want to wear your clothes in the farrowing house. The smell will stick to you," she said, good-naturedly. "And, I got to warn you, we've had city folks not be able to take the smell and get sick."

The Roush boys' hog operation tumbled out in a series of pens and sheds behind the family home. The farrow house was our first stop. Jack ran in eagerly and was in absolute awe of the giant sows in the pens on either side of him. I was nearly stopped dead by the smell, but I did as Sue had counseled and kept on. Jack was unbothered, and he pressed up against a pen, where a half-dozen newborn piglets, as pink as bubblegum and each barely the size of a football, suckled on their mother's teats. Jack laughed as they tumbled among themselves for a better feeding position. When Kaden picked one up and put it in Jack's arms, my son's eyes widened in delight.

Hog farming is obviously not for the faint of heart or the weak of stomach, but as we followed Jesse and Kaden through the pens and listened to them explain the care and commerce that go into such an endeavor, I was mightily impressed. Sue stayed with us throughout the tour, beaming with pride for her boys and offering a couple of tidbits that indicated she provided more than simple encouragement. Her rotator cuff in both shoulders had required surgery, aggravated by the pulling and pushing that is part of mating two hogs. Her back, too, had needed an operation for a complicated injury she had suffered recovering a hog from a mud hole.

When we sat down for dinner, it did not take long for the conversation to return to football and the Redmen's prospects against La Crosse. Sue Roush was a knowledgeable and devoted football fan; the "NFL Ticket" package that the family subscribed to from their satellite television company was for her. She had asked her husband and boys for it. Her oldest son had played for Coach Barta as well, and she knew the Redmen's lingo and philosophies, and she probably could have called a scoring drive from the sidelines if the coaching staff handed her a headset and playbook.

Sue looked forward to Friday nights. She shed her work clothes, put on earrings and a stepping-out outfit, and joined the rest of the town getting lost in Smith Center football. She had already spoken with Don Wick, whom Coach Barta had sent to scout the St. Francis–La Crosse game. She waited until Jesse and Kaden left the kitchen and then dropped into a whisper.

"Don says they are really, really good," she said, "that the game wasn't really as close as the score. He said they ran all over St. Francis."

The buzz had already started. On the *Topeka Capital-Journal*'s prepzone.com, a thread asking once more "Does the Streak End?" was launched soon after the St. Francis–La Crosse game. The back-and-forth on the board this time, however, was more reasoned. This was a big game that many people wanted to see, and only the most partisan were willing to go out on a limb to pick a winner.

"La Crosse scares me because they have excellent skill players. I don't know about their line," wrote a poster named Wardog, embodying the big-game respect that was being given to both teams. "SC would scare me for the simple fact if they want to they can keep the ball for a whole quarter. If SC controls the line of scrimmage they will win the game. On the other hand I don't know if they can have many empty trips, they need to take time and score.

"Musil is the real deal, but the one I would be concerned

about is the quarterback. Talk about putting pressure on the corners. SC will also do a better job of flowing to the ball then SF did, they were not real quick, SC is much quicker."

There was great anticipation in town, but it was met with an equal dose of apprehension. The Redmen were not a lock to make what was supposed to be a good team look bad, as they had done in the previous four seasons. They could lose, and this doubt manifested itself in unaccustomed ways.

In the *Echo*, Ivan Burgess was unable to tap into his usual brio about the dominance of all things Smith Center. "I hope Smith Center has their Casablanca defense going full blast," he wrote. "You remember the movie 'Casablanca' whenever something happened the Chief of the French police would say, 'round up the usual suspects.' That's the way Smith Center will have to defend La Crosse. Whenever La Crosse snaps the ball, the Redmen will have to round up anybody that looks suspicious like he might be carrying the ball and not only tackle them but tackle them hard.

"I mean tackle them really hard," he continued. "I mean hit like Smith Center hits people."

And, for the first time since I had arrived in Smith Center, I was on unsure footing. Long before the season began, when I told Coach Barta that if the Redmen lost it might be better for the narrative of the book, I had meant it. I figured that I was nimble enough to recognize the teaching moment in the defeat and somehow could find the nobility in bouncing back from the disappointments of real life.

When the Redmen looked mortal and in danger of losing at Norton early in the season, I was not roiled internally at all. I had steeled myself to be objective. I had reminded myself that I could not play the games and that whatever was going to happen was out of my control.

I was here to write about a team, and a town.

As each day passed and I learned a little more about the players, and as I witnessed how Coach Barta and the coaching staff taught them, I understood a little more about why the Redmen were successful. It had helped me develop a neat little parlor trick that I performed for some of the fathers.

Before kickoff, I'd predict the final score of the game.

Shane McCall, John Terrill, and some others knew I was at the practices, watching game plans develop during the week and listening to the motivational buttons that the coaches were pushing in meetings and pep talks. When the Redmen played Ellis, for example, I said they were going to shut out the Railers 40–0. They did. I called the Colby game at 32–0, and they won, 40–0 again. I had been right around the final scores ever since. The point was that I was in command of my material.

Now, for the first time, I had to get command of my emotions. I had fallen into a routine that I was not ready to see end. I looked forward to going to practice every day. I liked listening to the coaches needle each other, as well as how they tried to impart certain values to the players at team meetings. I liked wandering the practice field, visiting with Coach Barta and Big Hutch—all the coaches—and with Morse Boucher, Bill Rempe, and whoever else was around.

I liked the players, too. Over the months, our relationship had evolved from guarded "yes, sirs" and hesitant one-sentence answers to an easy dialogue. We had gotten to know each other's families. I had ridden their combines, visited their hog farms, and shared meals with them.

My son, Jack, had already been treated to a lifetime of kindness. He had been on a four-wheeler and in a chicken coop. He was swooped in the air, given high-fives, and had his hair tousled. He had discovered his first role models on the practice field, often riding atop Brock Hutchinson's shoulders or in the back of the panel water truck. Jack carried the Redmen's pads and fetched their water.

"Are we going to practice today, Dad?" he asked every morning.

When I picked Jack up from school, he insisted we stop and buy snacks for the "water boys." At home, Jack would get in a three-point stance, call out "Down. Set. Go," and then yell just like the Redmen did when they were doing sprints. He bounced from the dining room table to the couch to the easy chair, yelling, "hit, hit, hit," as if he were in line with them for the blocking sled.

Not only did Jack know every call-and-response verse of the Redmen's chant, "Everywhere we go, people want to know," but he sang it loud and proud while doing the same lunge stretches he had watched the team do to the song each day at practice.

As the big game with La Crosse approached, I knew the truth. I wanted the Redmen to crush the Leopards. I wanted them to win the whole championship and set the winning streak record.

The Smith Center Redmen had become "our boys," too.

# 15

I can't say this enough: You must know where 56 is.
He is the key player that takes you to the ball.

—Brock Hutchinson, November 10, 2008

A steady rain fell from dark clouds, submerging an already underwater practice field. Inside the Hubbard football complex, Coach Barta did not have his full team. He was missing eleven of his players, including most of his starting backfield. Marshall, the Rempes, and eight others were in Osborne performing in a vocal concert as members of the Chansonaires. These were not the ideal conditions for preparing for the toughest game of the season.

The lights were off, and the La Crosse–St. Francis film was projected on the screen. Coach Barta's unmistakable silhouette—arms crossed over cascading stomach—formed an eclipse over the flickering images.

"Biggest game of the year, and these guys are off at a music concert," he said in an irritated grumble. "They didn't even ask the music teacher if they really had to go."

Coach Barta ran a hand over his face.

"You guys make sure the ones who are missing get these scouting reports and study them," he said.

He paused again and then slipped back into an irritated growl.

"You young'uns, you listen up and study, too. I don't care who we're playing, you guys will get the snaps if the singers don't have a good week of practice."

On the laps of the Redmen was a twenty-two-page scouting report of the La Crosse team that Coach Barta and his staff believed was the Rosetta Stone for defeating the Leopards. The staff had spent nine hours in the NASA Lab on Sunday identifying offensive and defensive keys and finding weaknesses to attack when the Redmen traveled south on Friday to play La Crosse. Tim Lambert, the St. Francis coach, was in town for his grandmother's funeral, and Mike Rogers had asked him to stop by to be debriefed by the coaches. Tim marveled how the whole staff was on hand, and at the time and care they took looking at the film.

As far as La Crosse went, Tim said the better team had won. His kids had played hard but were not as fast as the Leopards. St. Francis lost the game on the big plays that La Crosse ran to the outside; his kids just couldn't get there. Coach Barta agreed. Of what he had seen, the Leopards were blessed with speed at all the skill positions. Jeremy Garcia was the best quarterback they had seen all year, completing 64 percent of his passes for more than 1,000 yards. Cory Torrez and Scot Irvin were burners at wide receiver. In the backfield, Marcus Moeder was a 142-pound tailback who had gained nearly 900 yards simply by running past people.

Then there was Marshall Musil. He had gained 1,067 yards because he was fast and powerful. He could catch and averaged better than fifteen yards a reception. He blocked like a road grader and was responsible not only for his accomplishments but also for Moeder's yards and often for

Garcia's time in the pocket. He was smart, too. Marshall's late father, Terry Musil, had coached down the road at Osborne, and Coach Barta had known and liked him very much. Terry had died from cancer when Marshall was a little boy. Coach Barta had gotten to see Marshall at track meets, and he was impressed with the young man and how his mother, Connie, and sister, Meredith, had formed a tight unit around him.

Coach Barta had heard that Marshall had attended summer camps at the University of Oklahoma, and that the Sooners' coaching staff knew immediately that they had a future "H-back" in their midst. From what he had seen, Coach Barta agreed: Marshall Musil was strong, athletic, and smart. He also had the coach's son's knack of not making mistakes.

The Leopards' coach, Ryan Cornelsen, was also a coach's son. His father, Gary, had won four state championships at Liberal High School in southwestern Kansas, and Ryan had put together a 51–13 record over six seasons at La Crosse. Just thirty-six years old, Cornelsen was confident and enthusiastic and straightforward enough to approach Coach Barta and Big Hutch at a state coaching convention to ask to pick their brains. It is a common practice in the coaching fraternity, and Coach Barta and Big Hutch were flattered. So in a hotel room in Wichita, Cornelsen played game film of the Redmen offense and asked them how they would stop their own offense. They liked his boldness.

"Name your damn poison," Big Hutch remembered telling him.

Then they proceeded to run down the different defenses they had encountered over the past thirty years, and how they had steamrolled them anyway. Coach Barta and Big Hutch knew that it was likely they would face La Crosse again. It didn't matter. They had enjoyed the session, admired Cornelsen's passion, and believed he was going to be a terrific coach for years to come.

When Coach Barta sat at the computer earlier in the afternoon to draft the theme for this week of preparation, he was revved up. Coaching in big games, finding weaknesses on film, and exploiting them on the field were among the most gratifying parts of his profession. He knew exactly what points he needed to emphasize to his players.

1. We have a game. You must get ready. A real test.
2. They are a big strong team. We must use our speed, quickness, and toughness. Hit them.

He also knew how to take apart the Leopards. It was all there in those twenty-two pages, and his staff was jazzed about it, especially Brock. Little Hutch saw the keys to shutting down La Crosse's high flying offense so clearly that here on Monday he was already in his evangelical pregame mode.

"We've done the heavy lifting all year, gentlemen," he said. "We have worked hard. This is a mental week, a week where we are going to keep our head in the game and out-think our opponents. You're going to study. Out on the practice field, we're going to recognize things and talk to each other.

"By Friday night, I guarantee you that we will know where they are going before the ball is snapped. Very simply, gentleman, you need to know where no. 2 and no. 56 are because they will lead you to the play. So, listen up."

Over the next two hours, Brock was in rapture as the film raced forward and backward, play after play, demonstrating his insight that Marshall Musil and the left guard,

Clinton Kershner, would lead the Redmen to the ball every time. The Leopards, indeed, depended on Kershner to be the lead blocker on virtually every running play. Sometimes, they pulled him; other times, they flipped him to the right side of the line. No matter where he started, the ball always followed.

"I can't say this enough: You must know where 56 is," Brock said, loud enough that it echoed in the locker room. "He is the key player that takes you to the ball."

And time after time on the white screen, either Musil followed Kershner, or Garcia kept the ball, or Garcia handed it to Moeder. Either way, both followed Musil, who was following Kershner.

There was more. Whenever Musil lined up in the slot or as a receiver, Garcia was going to try to pass to him. The film did not lie. It showed Musil going wide and then catching a pass. When Musil got a handoff in the backfield, he always hesitated and drifted east or west until he spotted a lane that he could motor through.

"We're going to be coming for Musil, and we're going to wrap him up while he's standing there trying to go sideways," Brock said.

"Watch him," he commanded. Once more the film was telling the story. "When he finds a hole and gets his shoulders square, he's dangerous. We're not going to let him square his shoulders. Are we?"

"No, sir," yelled the Redmen, now caught up in Brock's cadence.

On it went, the flaws and tipoffs in the Leopards' offense, pointed out and shown over and over again on screen. Moeder did not like to run inside. He didn't like getting hit. So the Redmen were going to fly from the corners and turn him into the middle. They were going to hit him. Hard. The quarterback, Garcia, liked to run the ball himself on short yardage up between the tackle and end, and especially near the goal line.

"He tips off every time," said Mike Rogers, from his chair in the back of the room. "Watch his right foot when he gets under center."

"See, right there," he said. The film was paused. "He drops that right foot back, getting ready to go."

What La Crosse intended to do on defense was even clearer to the Redmen coaching staff. The Leopards had played St. Francis the week before, after all, and had done a decent job of shutting down an offense that was identical to Smith Center's. They did it by dropping a "monster back" behind the nose guard; he was going to shoot the gaps on either side of the center and free up Musil, who played middle linebacker, to chase the ball and make plays. They also moved Garcia, who played outside linebacker, closer to the line. He was going to bolt between the guard and the tackle in an effort to blow up the play in the backfield immediately after the handoff.

Coach Barta thought his kids were stronger and faster than St. Francis's; La Crosse would be unable to stop the Redmen offense.

When the lights came on, Coach Barta got to his feet.

"You can see we had a good day breaking down film yesterday," he said. "It took us all day, and when Coach Lambert of St. Francis stopped by, he was impressed about how hard these guys were working on a Sunday. I am blessed that I have the coaches I have."

Coach Barta made eye contact with Big Hutch, Mike, Brock, and Tim.

"I know they do it for all of you," he said. "They do it because they love you."

Coach Barta glanced at his notes.

"Shawn's dad had a heart attack, and he's had a rough go of it," he said, referring to the father of Shawn Stansbury, a junior who probably would play quarterback for the Redmen the following year.

"Let's keep him in our prayers," the coach said. "Now go home. It's too wet, and I don't want to get anyone hurt. I'm sure some of you will get these scouting reports to the guys that were missing."

With no reason for a shower, the locker room was empty within moments. The coaches, too, had gotten out quickly—all except for Coach Barta and Brock. When I asked Coach Barta if he had really been blindsided by so many of his players going to the concert in Osborne, he laughed.

"Hell, no," he said. "I knew about it. When it gets late in the year, sometimes you have to manufacture a little controversy. The kids down there are some of our smartest and most dedicated. They'll know all this stuff by practice tomorrow."

"It's probably better that their minds are off football," said Brock. "Let them forget about it for a day, and they'll be more fresh."

Both were aware this was the biggest football game western Kansas had seen in a long time. They had listened to the radio, watched the message boards, and heard the talk around town. When I asked Coach Barta if he had the same hunch he had before the Norton game, that the Redmen were about to be in a tough game, he let out a good-natured sigh.

"Oh, Joe, I don't know," he said in a tone that I had heard before from him, also from the character Eeyore in

*Winnie-the-Pooh*. It was forlorn and singsong, and always made me smile.

"You never know if this is the game you're going to get beat, and you really can't worry about it," he said. "It took me a long time to figure that out. I'd get all worked up, and we'd lose, and then I'd feel lower than whale shit."

Brock laughed.

"It sounds like someone else we know," he said.

"Yeah, Brooks," said Coach Barta, chuckling.

He had spent many Friday nights on the phone with his son after Brooks's team lost a game. "He thinks he's the worst coach in the world, and wants to quit every time he loses."

"Who'd he get that from?" Brock asked.

Coach Barta chuckled again.

"We play our game, Coach," said Brock. "We're twenty-four points better than them."

Coach Barta did not disagree.

For the next three days, the Redmen gave a clinic on what "good on good" meant to Smith Center football. Kris Lehmann had dropped the scouting reports off to the teammates who had attended the concert, and Marshall, Travis, Trevor, and the rest had done their homework. Whenever the Black Shirts got into a La Crosse formation, Logan Tuxhorn, Colt, and Kris would shout out where "no. 56" was and what was coming. Matt Atwood played Marshall Musil and took an absolute beating from the starters. Matt was two hundred pounds of muscle who was going to play a lot the following season at fullback. He gave as good as he got, and the hardest hitting I saw during practice all season was when Matt was playing Musil.

At a team meeting on the eve of the game, Mike Rogers reminded the team that in the mid-1990s the Redmen had defeated Victoria High School, a team that had a Division I prospect named Monty Beisel, who now played in the NFL for the Arizona Cardinals.

"Marshall Musil is going to Oklahoma," he said. "We all know that. But those are the guys you want to play against. You will remember playing against him for the rest of your life. You'll be reminded of it on Saturdays over the next four years when Oklahoma is on television, and maybe even on Sundays for a while after that.

"I know there are guys in town who still see Monty Beisel on TV and tell their buddies, 'Hey, we beat him up in high school.' This is your chance, and frankly, guys, this is the best team you're going to play. You know the saying 'Christmas came early'? Well, it's true in this case. This is the state championship game. The winner tomorrow is going to bring the trophy home. You can bet on it."

———

The La Crosse players had been gracious in their pregame public remarks about the Redmen, and they understood how much it meant to their town that they were facing Smith Center in a game of this magnitude. In fact, the school was putting up temporary grandstand seating for an additional 1,500 people.

"It is the biggest game in La Crosse High School history," Jeremy Garcia told the *Hays Daily News*. "It's exciting. I am part of it. My friends are part of it. I am the starting quarterback. It is really exciting, it really is. We are expecting a big crowd. I hope we do well."

Coach Cornelsen was lavish in his praise of the Smith Center coaching staff and the program's accomplishments.

"I think it is the fact that they have eleven good football

players on the field at all times," he told the newspaper. "That is tough for schools our size and schools that are 2A to do. A lot of teams will get the best kids they can get, but are not necessarily great football players. Since I have seen them play the last four years, they don't have a weak spot.

"They don't have a kid that you can attack. They don't have an area that doesn't look good. They can stop the pass, they can stop the run. That's tough to do at small schools where you can keep getting guys over and over that can get it done. I would say that is probably their biggest strength."

La Crosse, like every good team in western Kansas, had been pointing to this game since long before the season started. Last summer, Morse Boucher had been in a check-out line at the Walmart in Hays when a kid saw that he was wearing a Smith Center hat.

"We're going to beat you this year," said the young man, who was wearing a La Crosse T-shirt.

In the past three seasons, the Leopards had compiled a 32–2 record with one of those losses a 46–0 drubbing by Smith Center in the 2006 playoffs. This year they were 11–0 and ranked no. 2 in the state behind the Redmen. The Leopards believed they were the right team to snap the winning streak and Smith Center's grip on the state title. They, too, believed this was the real state championship game.

The population of La Crosse—1,376—had quadrupled on game night. Its stadium did not have much parking, and folks were pulling into spaces wherever in town they found them, and hiking to the lights that loomed east of Main Street. It didn't matter that it was a bitterly cold night; the grandstands were packed, and the people were three deep all the way around the field's perimeter.

The Redmen, of course, had been here since 5:10 p.m., sprawled across the La Crosse gym floor and sinking into their iPods, readying themselves for a game they could not wait to play. Dillon Corbett, however, had gotten restless and wandered into the Leopards' weight room. Dillon was one of the stalwarts of the offensive and defensive lines. He blew holes open for the backs on offense and made plays from his position as defensive end. Dillon was one of the happy-go-lucky juniors; they were everything the seniors weren't—extremely confident.

A document caught Dillon's attention on the floor in the weight room: La Crosse's scouting report of Smith Center. Inside, there were a few pages of data and very cursory observations that would not even have made it into the Redmen's scouting reports. It was the cover that was interesting. There was an illustration of what looked like a state championship ring and a message typed out under the headline, WE WILL PLAY WITH A PASSION ABOVE ALL EXPECTATIONS.

"Smith Center creates an image on the countless radio, T.V. Stations and even a book about them, that they're real humble, classy football program and team," it began. "They've proved to me several times in the last six years that this is a cover for the real personalities."

Coach Cornelsen's tirade was just getting started. The preamble on the scouting report took the Redmen to task for arrogant behavior at the previous spring's track meets, and accused the coaching staff of routinely running up the score on opponents to show their dominance. He claimed that the Redmen coaches made fun of the teams they played at the film session he had with them at the clinic in Wichita. He accused the Redmen players and their parents of being incessant trash talkers. Coach Cornelsen claimed that he was not alone in his feelings, that every school that the Redmen played felt the same way.

Coach Cornelsen wrote that what bothered him the most was that Smith Center's coaching staff, players—the whole town—were phonies, and had suckered the media into portraying them as humble when they were anything but.

"I'm tired of their cocky attitudes, disrespect and the image they try to portray," he wrote. "Let's find out how humble they are when they get knocked around, and they are on the loosing [sic] side."

Dillon was more amused by this bulletin-board fodder than made angry by it. He was laughing as he passed it around. But Marshall, Kris, Trenton, Trevor, and Travis were steamed. Word of the scouting report spread through the room like a nasty virus. When Coach Barta finally heard about it, he took it away without reading it. He could tell his team didn't need any more motivation.

Brock was briefer than he had been all season. "You know that Coach has taught you guys to win with class," he said. "Let's go out there and show them why we are champions."

To get to the field from their locker room, the Redmen parted hundreds of La Crosse fans through a gap in the home team's grandstands. They paired off and clasped hands. They seemed to get bigger as they passed through the hostile territory. There was not a trace of nervous energy as they took the field for the opening kickoff.

The first minute of the game set the tone for the next forty-seven. On the second play from scrimmage at the Redmen's own 8-yard line, Joe Osburn took the ball from Travis and followed a devastating block by Cody Tucker, bounced to the Smith Center sideline, and then went ninety-two yards for the touchdown. The Redmen's whole bench provided an out-of-bounds convoy for him into the end zone. It set off a cathartic celebration in the Smith Center grandstands and left the Leopard faithful silent and out of breath.

La Crosse's fans came to life again after the kickoff when the Leopards' offense took the field. This unit was averaging more than fifty points a game—surely they would answer the Redmen's opening salvo. As Garcia led the Leopards to the line of scrimmage, Marshall McCall tapped Trevor on the rump and nodded resolutely at Kris.

When the ball was snapped, he zeroed in on Marshall Musil, who had the ball and was drifting left. Trevor had him at the thighs, and Marshall McCall lowered his head and suddenly felt like he had been fired from a slingshot. The collision was brutal. Marshall had buried Musil for a two-yard loss.

La Crosse went three plays and was forced to punt. Travis Rempe was smiling as he led the Redmen offense onto the field.

"Deep-breathe on three," he said. The practice had become the Redmen's mantra, a call to relax and go to work. Travis handed the ball to his brother four straight times, each of them ending the same way—with Trevor dragging La Crosse tacklers into the center of the field. Now that the middle was soft, Travis handed the ball to Colt, who scooted off tackle between Justin and Kris and was in the end zone fifty yards later. Just like that, the score was Redmen 12, Leopards 0.

After forcing La Crosse to punt again, Smith Center looked to close the door for good. Instead, Colt lost the punt in the lights, and the ball bounced off his shoulder pads. The Leopards recovered it at the Smith Center 9-yard line. Colt hung his head, and on the sidelines his father, Mike, did the same. On third and goal, Jeremy Garcia hit Corey Torrez on a slant pattern for a seven-yard score, cutting the lead to 12–6 after Musil's kick failed.

As the Redmen huddled near midfield, Colt came running in from one end, and Mike approached from the other end. No one was sure what kind of explosion to expect.

"That's on me," Colt said. "It won't happen again."

"Forget about it, Colt," said Mike.

He patted his son on the helmet.

"Nobody is hurt," Mike said. "Let's go get another one."

That is what the Redmen did. They took their time, going sixty-nine yards over thirteen plays. Trevor Rempe again was the workhorse, and he showed the Leopards how a fullback runs from the textbook. He took nine handoffs up the middle, his legs never stopping, and his helmet bashing into Musil, Garcia, and whoever else got in his way. When he took the ball into the end zone from the 1-yard line, it was Trevor's thirty-eighth yard on the drive and he looked as strong as he did when the game began.

The Redmen defense was even better. Brock had dissected La Crosse perfectly. Marshall and Kris Lehmann were following the guard Kershner and delivering knee-wobbling hits on Garcia, Musil, and Moeder. Dillon, Trevor, and Joel Osburn were getting to Musil in the backfield as he moved laterally, never letting him get his shoulders squared. Whenever the Leopards got the tiniest bit of offensive traction, the Redmen came up with big plays. On consecutive drives, spanning the second and third quarters, La Crosse reached the Redmen's 31-, 26-, 36-, and 11-yard lines before having to give up the ball on downs.

No one knew better how dominating the Redmen defense was than Marshall Musil. After forty-eight minutes of football, the best running back in Kansas and future Oklahoma Sooner had gained just twenty-one yards and his high school career ended without a state title in a 32–14 loss. He led the Leopards across the field to shake hands and, after making it halfway through the line, couldn't help himself.

"What! Are there like three thousand of you guys?" he said. "It felt like that all night. Everywhere I went, one of you guys was on me."

When he reached the end of the line, Coach Barta reached out his right hand and stretched his left arm up to touch Musil's shoulder pad. "I knew your father, and he was a really good man," he told Musil. "I know how proud he is of you as a football player, and as a man. Good luck at Oklahoma."

# 16

You have done a heck of a job writing the final chapter to this book.

—Darren Sasse, November 21, 2008

"I guess you liked Coach Cornelsen more than he liked you," said Big Hutch before practice the following Monday.

Brock, Mike, and Tim joined in the laughter. The La Crosse scouting report had been left on a desk in the coaches' office.

"I thought we got along," said Coach Barta, smiling.

"He didn't know one of his kids was going to leave it lying around," Brock said. "He didn't do anything wrong. It was good motivation. And, Dad, you're the arrogant one he's talking about."

"I figured it was me," said Big Hutch, pausing. "I told him the truth. Our offense is impossible to stop."

There were no hard feelings. Ryan Cornelsen wanted to fire up his team. It was a young coach's mistake, however, to put it in writing and leave it in the hands of teenagers.

Coach Barta was far subtler when it came to motivation. He adhered to the "respect everybody but fear no one" creed that he laid down in every preseason. He tried to frame opponents as the antagonists. This Friday, for example, the Redmen were going to the other end of Kansas to play Meade for the substate championship, which is one level below the Kansas state title game. The Buffaloes' team motto is: WHEN YOU ARE THE HAMMER, EVERYTHING LOOKS LIKE A NAIL. So it got top billing in the scouting report. The Buffaloes were big up front; their linemen averaged 240 pounds. Their only loss had been to La Crosse, though it was a bad one, 51–7, and that was perhaps balanced by the fact that the Buffaloes had defeated 10–1 Ellis handily, 20–8, in the previous playoff round.

Meade ran the single wing, which, like the Barta-Bone, teams did not see very often. In fact, the last time the Redmen faced the single wing it was in the 2001 semifinal game, and Conway Springs sent them home. The single wing is an offense that relies on tricking and finessing the defense, rather than overpowering them. None other than Glenn "Pop" Warner was its original architect. It usually starts with a long snap from center to one of four backs, which include a tailback, a fullback, a quarterback who often blocks, and a wingback. Down front, there are two linemen on one side and four on the other side of the center.

Coach Barta knew his defense especially had a lot of work ahead of them to get used to seeing the single wing. He believed Meade was going to cause problems early as the Redmen got used to finding the ball. The coach was not going to look past these problems, but he simply did not believe that the Buffaloes were better than his team.

Coach Barta was more concerned about the logistics of getting to Meade, which is 250 miles south of Smith Center and about 45 miles from the Oklahoma border. He had the option of playing the game on Saturday, which would mean driving down on Friday and staying the night. Coach Barta wanted no part of that. In 1993, the Redmen had driven down and spent the night in Elkhart, in the southwest corner of the state, for a Saturday afternoon playoff game. They played so poorly—and got beat—that Coach Barta swore not to do that ever again if he could help it.

Therefore, he was going to keep the game on Friday night and prepare his boys for a nine-hour round-trip. The folks at Meade were going to feed the boys, win or lose, before sending them back to Smith Center.

"It probably is going to be twelve hours, the way we have to stop all the time so you can go to the bathroom," he told Big Hutch.

The schedule meant the bus would leave at nine thirty in the morning and stop for lunch in Hays, and perhaps again in Dodge City, so the Redmen could stretch their legs. It wasn't the ideal way to prepare for a game.

"It's too much road and too much waiting around," he told his coaches, "but I don't have any better ideas."

Coach Barta was also very conscious of not pushing his team too hard in the coming week, especially mentally. The Redmen had absorbed a lot of information and had controlled their fury beautifully in preparation for La Crosse. Still, it had been a taxing game, emotionally as well as physically. The Redmen had now played eleven games, and the championship, the game that mattered most, was still a week away.

"We can't squeeze that motivational lemon dry, yet," Coach Barta told his coaches. "We just want to make sure they're ready to play and that they know that they are a better team than Meade."

There also was the matter of how to address the winning streak with his team. A victory over the Buffaloes would tie the record of sixty-six games, set by the Panthers of Pittsburg Colgan. Reporters from around the state were beginning to call, because it was the Redmen who had snapped the Panthers' streak in the 2004 state championship game. On Friday, Pittsburg Colgan was playing Olpe in the other semifinal game.

"It's a neat story if we see them in the title game, and they have a chance to stop us at sixty-six," offered Mike Rogers.

"We haven't said anything all year about it," Coach Barta said. "Let's not start now. And believe me, if we get Colgan next week, that's all we're going to hear about. Let's win our game, first."

The Redmen, indeed, looked tired most of the week, but they never gave the impression that they were taking Meade for granted. When coaches from Tabor College showed up one afternoon to watch the seniors, the intensity level spiked and the hitting got much more focused. Even Trenton Terrill, who had just come back from his knee ligament tear to play special teams against La Crosse, was flying all over the practice field. He had only two more football games to play, but apparently he still wanted to make an impression.

Joe Osburn met with the coaches from Tabor. He was the senior most coveted by recruiters because he was simply the best all-around athlete. He had more than 1,200 rushing yards and twelve touchdowns. Joe was also a solid cornerback, kick returner, and punter. But he was the least interested in attending college, especially since he was struggling once more in the classroom. His English class was reading *Macbeth* aloud and then being quizzed on it, and Joe wasn't getting it. Kris Lehmann was in his class, however, and he was doing his best to explain Shakespeare to Joe.

When policing the team required finesse, that task usually fell to Kris, Trenton, and Marshall. All three had just made the honor roll, and Trenton and Marshall had just made the superintendent's list, which meant that they had a grade-point average higher than 3.5.

Joe would have made the superintendent's list if *Mario Kart* on the Xbox was a course of study. He was as slippery at video games as he was on the football field. He was also just as frustrating for those trying to help him. Coach Barta had tried taking a hard line and a soft line with him. Joe was gentle to the point of passivity, which tried his teammates' patience even more.

Either Joe was going to buckle down and learn his *Macbeth*, or he was not. The proof would be in the upcoming quizzes.

Coach Barta had received some other news that had shaken him up. Tom Bowen, a former basketball coach and teacher at Ellis and Colby, had died. He was sixty-three—just like Coach Barta—and had recently retired to move to Wichita to be near his daughters and grandchildren. The two coaches had come up together.

"It reminds you of how old you are and makes you think about what you're doing," Coach Barta said. "We coached against each other, and he was a real good guy. His retirement sure didn't last long."

The coach was adept at dodging questions about when he was going to retire. He liked his current arrangement, which kept him on the sidelines, out of the classroom, and allowed him plenty of time to travel and see his grandchildren, which he did a lot in the off-season. Another reason he did not like talking about hanging it up was because a discussion of his likely successor soon followed. As impossible as he would be to replace, there was a bounty of qualified candidates. The problem was that many of them were on his staff. Only Big Hutch was not in contention. Mike, Brock, Tim, and Darren Sasse were as good as anyone in the state and had already turned down other jobs.

None of them was going anywhere. How could Coach Barta choose one over another? The conjecture around town was that the early favorite to replace him was Tim Lambert at St. Francis because it would eliminate that hard decision. Not only was Tim a former Redman, but it could be argued that he was the most qualified because he had already spent sixteen years as a head coach.

Coach Barta didn't seem to be in a great hurry to quit coaching. He was only thirteen wins short of three hundred victories. If the Redmen kept winning, Coach Barta would reach that milestone in the playoffs next year. It also was unlikely that he would walk away while the streak was intact. The current juniors and sophomores were potentially far more talented than Marshall, Kris, the Rempes, and the rest of the seniors. Among Colt Rogers, Dillon Corbett, Logan Tuxhorn, Jesse Roush, and Matt Atwood, there was an experienced core in the junior class. The McNary twins, Willie Overmiller, and Van Tucker were exceptional sophomores. Coach Barta refused to compare classes, but his eyes twinkled when he was asked about the future.

"We got some pretty good kids coming up," he said.

Tom Bowen's death also reminded me of what seventy-nine-year-old Florida State coach Bobby Bowden once told me was the reason that he stayed on the sidelines. "When you retire, there is just one more big event," Bowden said. "And I ain't ready for that."

I suspected Coach Barta had a similar fear.

———

Before the Meade game, the Redmen looked like a team that had been on a bus for six hours. Trevor Rempe, who usually sat and stewed himself into a rage, paced between the locker room and the gymnasium. He was restless, and there was too much time to kill. Lunch at the Pizza Hut in Hays had not taken as long as they planned, and the team was here by 4:30 p.m.

Win or lose, Trevor had a busy weekend planned. The school play, *Virgil's Family Reunion*, debuted Saturday and was to be performed again on Sunday, and he had the second biggest role as Virgil's best friend, Ellard. It was always hard for me to reconcile Trevor's pregame scowl with the easy smile he wore on stage and every other time I saw him.

It was another bitterly cold night, and the field at Meade sat atop a plateau, so there was no place to hide from the wind. The stadium was full, with perhaps four thousand people, but the stands sat far back from the field and the game seemed to unfold in silence. The Redmen were listless even as they forced Meade to punt on their opening drive. Then Joe Osburn heated things up with a thirty-nine-yard burst to the Meade 30-yard line. The Redmen pounded their way to a score over the next five plays, with Colt taking the ball in for a touchdown from the 4-yard line. When Joe ran in the two-point conversion, the Redmen had an 8–0 lead, but they still had not woken up.

There was no pad pounding on the sidelines, no ecstatic

huddle on the field. The Redmen offense just waltzed off the field as if they had done this before, which they had, and were certain they would get an opportunity to do it some more.

Instead, Meade answered with a methodical ten-play drive whose pace and strength seemed to be lifted from the Smith Center script. The Redmen defense was having trouble finding the ball. When they did, the Buffaloes' running backs Eddie Beachy, Taylor Headrick, and Dakota Benear were already four or five yards downfield. The Meade linemen were smothering Trevor and Justin inside and hiding the running backs from Kris, Joel, and Logan. They were big, especially Skyler Avis (six foot three, 265 pounds), Trevin Pfanenstiel (six foot two, 315 pounds), and Tanner Wiens (six foot four, 220 pounds). No one had moved the ball on the Redmen like that this year, and the drive burned time off the clock. When Headrick scored from the 1-yard line and then carried in the two-point conversion, there was only 1:28 remaining in the first quarter, and the score was tied at 8–8.

The Redmen sideline finally came alive on the next series when Colt jitterbugged fifty-eight yards for a touchdown. It was his twenty-third scoring run of the year, and though the runs all looked alike, they never got boring to watch. Colt got the ball, and then you'd lose sight of him as he ran between his blockers. He would then duck an arm tackle, spin and squirt through another crowd and to the sideline, and then cross up the last defender with an inside cut. Colt ran as if he were fastened to tracks on the field, like those slot car sets you played with as a kid.

When the Redmen snuffed another drive, Meade's Taylor Headrick let fly with a picture-perfect forty-six-yard punt that landed inside the 10-yard line and then rolled out of bounds at about the one-inch line. It was a thing of beauty. Shane McCall, John Terrill, and the whole Smith Center stats crew could not suppress their admiration.

"Whoa, can you believe it?" asked Shane with a grin.

"What a kick," echoed John, who had his headset on and was doing the play-by-play.

The Buffaloes were too eager to make a big play and jumped off-side before the first snap, so the ball was moved out to the 6-yard line. Trevor banged inside for nine yards and then got five more yards on the next play. One play later, Joe followed Van and Cody Tucker on the right side, then rocketed to the sideline and took the ball sixty-five yards for the touchdown.

The score was 22–8 with 7:28 left in the first half, and a pattern had been established. Meade mounted long, time-killing drives; the Redmen scored quickly. The Buffaloes knew they had to keep Smith Center off the field if they were to have a chance at the upset. From its own 36-yard line, Meade revved up their single wing offense. They took three yards here, four yards there, and moved the sticks, converting one first down after another. Taylor Headrick was doing most of the damage, slipping beneath his big blockers on six consecutive plays until the Buffaloes were on the Redmen's 1-yard line. The problem, however, was the clock was running out on the first half and Meade did not have any time-outs. As time ticked down—eight, seven, six—it appeared that Smith Center would get to the locker room without letting the Buffaloes score.

"Time-out, time-out," screamed Brock Hutchinson.

He was four yards onto the field, waving his arms to get the referees' attention. Logan, Kris, Marshall—the whole Redmen defensive unit—were looking at him. They were confused about what scheme Brock had called. The Buffaloes, hurrying to run one last play before the half, had panicked the Redmen.

"What in the hell are you doing?" Coach Barta barked at Brock. "Get your head in the game."

Brock had lost track of the clock. There was no way Meade would have gotten another play off if Brock had not called for the time-out. Now they were guaranteed a shot at the end zone. The extra minutes allowed the Buffaloes' coaching staff enough time to decide which play would be most effective. Brock knew he had made a mistake. He gathered his defense, told them what formation he wanted, and sent them back on the field. And then Brock watched from the sidelines as Headrick powered over the right side for a touchdown as the clock expired. Brock dropped his head. He left it there as the Buffaloes tried, and failed, to convert their two-point attempt. The score was now 22–14, and Meade had momentum.

Those were the first angry words exchanged between coaches I had heard all season. But by the time the Redmen crossed the field and got to the locker room, they were forgotten. Coach Barta huddled outside with his coaches.

"Here's the problem," he said, pounding a clipboard that had the statistics from the first half.

Inside, the Redmen were pulling on water bottles and burying their fists in hand warmers. They looked neither tired nor perplexed. They watched Coach Barta walk in and waited for their coach's words.

"This is one of those strange games, guys," he said. "We have scored every time we've had the ball. They can't stop us. At the same time, we're not doing a very good job of stopping them. We're not seeing the ball, and I was afraid of that. This statistic right here tells us everything we need to know. They have run forty-one offensive plays. We've only run sixteen. I guess we're going to have to outscore them."

As Meade kicked off to start the second half, the Buffaloes' coach, Scott Moshier, caught the Redmen napping with an onside kick. The ball tumbled to the Smith Center 46-yard line, where there was a scramble and then a scrum. As the pile untangled, Meade's Brian Deighton bounced up with the ball. Suddenly, the Meade faithful were on their feet and into the game. For a brief moment, Smith Center looked mortal, and it was up to the Buffaloes to take advantage.

Three times they flooded the right side with the single wing, only to be stopped after a couple of yards—first by Kris, then by Joel, and finally by Marshall. It was now fourth down, and the Buffaloes needed two yards. The ball went to Headrick once more, but this time Matt Atwood was right on top of him, picking him up like a runaway calf and dumping him on his back for a six-yard loss.

The Redmen were awake for good now, and they did what Coach Barta told them to do. They outscored the Buffaloes. The offense needed only seven minutes to score three touchdowns. Trevor rumbled for a fifteen-yard score, Joe scooted for fifty-one yards, and Joel Osburn scored from four yards out to make the score 44–14. Meade mounted a couple of long drives but could not get in the end zone. When Dereck McNary jetted to a forty-six-yard score with 3:08 to play, it was the offense's fifth consecutive possession to end in a touchdown.

The scoreboard read: Smith Center 60, Meade 14. The "66" placards were handed out in the Redmen's stands and then immediately held aloft until they formed a large mural of triumph. The Redmen now owned a share of the state record.

It was not only the Redmen's most impressive victory of the season, but one that showed how proficient, how dominating Smith Center had become. They ran only thirty-seven plays but gained 527 yards. Twenty-four plays were runs of more than five yards, and four of them went for more than forty-five yards. Meade, meanwhile, ran twice as many plays and gained fewer than half the yards.

"We're going to Hays," said Big Hutch, referring to Fort Hays State, where the title game is played. Then he walked down the sideline, shaking every player's hand. "Congratulations, men, we're going to Hays," he told them.

Logan Tuxhorn watched the celebration taking flight in the stands as the "66" placards danced in the air. "After next week, we're going to own that streak," he said. "I don't care who we play. I hope it's Colgan. I'd love to take the record from the team who had owned it."

There was another trophy to pick up for being substate champions and another photograph to be captured. Marshall, Kris, Trenton, and the rest of the seniors closed into a circle and hugged.

Soon, however, the Redmen were back in the Meade gym—two hundred or so coaches, players, and parents. This was a moment for the seniors. I watched them as they leaned into their moms and dads. They were proud, yet also tired and uncertain as to what the previous twelve weeks might have meant. They knew they had done something exceptional, but wanted to know exactly what.

They were boys, after all. The coaches could not quite get their arms around what exactly had happened, either.

Yet. They had not believed a date in the state title game was guaranteed, no matter their reputation.

"We get to play one more week, one more game," Coach Barta said. He reached for something else to say but could not find the words. "I'm so proud of you."

Big Hutch was even more tongue-tied. "It was a little scary in the first half," he admitted. "But in the second half you came out and did better."

"This has been one of the most exciting seasons we have had in quite a while," said Mike Rogers. He pulled Colt closer to him. "We had a lot of people step up," Mike went on, then swallowed. "It was fun to watch you grow."

It was Little Hutch's turn next. He got right down to it: "I'll be quite honest with you, we weren't very good early. Not very good at all. To see y'all now is something." He choked back a sob. "I've watched a lot of young boys grow up to be men. That's a tribute to all of your hard work."

When it was Tim Wilson's turn, he made sure to tell the Black Shirts that once more they had done a tremendous job preparing the varsity. Better than that, he reminded them, the Redmen had upheld another tradition: "There's two teams left, and that's the way we want it to be. It's a nice tradition to go to practice Thanksgiving morning and then eat turkey in the afternoon. Our last game will be our best game."

Finally, it was Darren Sasse's turn to put a postscript on the season. He usually was the most reserved on these occasions. But he knew better than most how far the senior class had come.

Not six years ago, they were runts and wannabes who were afraid of their own shadows. He used to tell Coach Barta and the rest of the coaches, "If only they could make some big plays and gain some confidence." Now, they had made plenty of big plays and were on the verge of doing something no one would have predicted: winning a state championship and doing it in convincing fashion.

"You have done a heck of a job writing the final chapter to this book," he said. "I . . . I . . . am proud of you."

# 17

We play this game today because you live in Smith Center, Kansas, in a community that loves you and watches over you. Each one of you was born to be Redmen.

—Brock Hutchinson, November 29, 2008

The bus did not arrive back from Meade until nearly three in the morning, and Coach Barta was in no shape to drive Saturday morning to exchange film with the coach from Olpe, Chris Schmidt. The Eagles had handled Pittsburg Colgan easily, 20–0, and were undefeated at 13–0. There would be no made-for-television-news story lines about two familiar foes, the Redmen and the Panthers, meeting to decide on the field which team had the best 2A program in Kansas. Still, someone had to exchange the film.

Pam Barta volunteered. The dropoff was in Salina, which was 125 miles away, halfway between Smith Center and Olpe, a crossroads community that was part of Emporia (population 26,639) in mid-eastern Kansas. Pam needed to shop for Christmas, and Salina offered a bevy of malls. She met the coach at Walmart.

"I hope we come out on top," she told him.

The Kansas playoffs were set up so the best team from the western part of the state met the best in the east. For

Smith Center, and any other town in western Kansas, they might as well have faced a team from Missouri. The eastern part of the state, with Kansas City, Topeka, and Wichita, was crowded and urban and held little attraction to folks here. They looked at it as a jumble of suburbs and frowned on its brand of football, which relied on passing and fancy offenses. It was a soft game, rather than the tough, hard-hitting style of play the Redmen and their faithful preferred.

At this point, all anyone knew about Olpe was what a statistics sheet and a feature story from the Emporia paper had sketched out. The Eagles averaged thirty-nine points a game and played what appeared to be an excellent defense: they had allowed an average of only four points a game; they had held St. Mary's, a traditional power, to seven points in the quarterfinals, and they had shut out Pittsburg Colgan. The last time Olpe had played for the state title was in 1976, when a half-dozen of the fathers of members of this current team also defeated Colgan in the semifinals. Their sons now were hoping to do what their daddies did not do thirty-two years ago: take the next step and win the championship.

In Smith Center, it did not matter what was going on in Olpe. A sense of joy, as well as inevitability, had settled throughout town. *Virgil's Family Reunion* drew standing-room-only crowds for both performances at the school auditorium. Many of the same folks who cheered on the football team on Friday nights had shown up to roar at the funny moments performed on stage by Smith Center's thespians. Most of the football players involved built props and were on the stage crew.

And Trevor Rempe was a revelation as Virgil's second banana and dim-witted friend. Trenton Terrill and Kaden

Roush hit their marks and delivered their lines with aplomb as well.

Greg Hobelmann had enlisted his wife, Peggy, to run the camera for him. He had been to Meade and back with his video crew as well, but he refused to miss the opportunity to capture any of the school performances. Greg wanted all the Smith Center students to get their star turns on Channel 17. Greg Koelsch also was roaming the wings and the auditorium. He, too, had bounced from one end of the state and back and looked wiped out.

Jack Benn had picked up an infection on the long drive back and forth to Meade and was bedridden and in danger of missing the championship game. He pulled himself out of bed long enough to commission Jim Fetters, a retired lawyer and hopelessly devoted musician, to record a song that Jack had penned. Jack was calling it "We Beat Everyone, Man," and it would be sung to the tune of Johnny Cash's "I've Been Everywhere" and would name the twenty-four different teams the Redmen had beaten over the span of their streak.

Even Coach Barta was exuberant—for him. He had the Olpe film rolling, but more as a backdrop than for breaking down. He moved quickly to the center of the locker room and spoke with passion.

"You're all coming back from Hays as state champions, or you're walking home," he said. "On that artificial turf down there you all ought to be quicker than snot."

He had a lot on his mind, and he rifled through it quickly.

"We're going to practice Thanksgiving Day in the morning, guys," he said. "At ten, which gives you plenty of time to be with your family in the afternoon. We're going to do the same thing Friday morning. We have a noon kickoff, and I want you used to being up and active at that hour. You understand me, guys."

Coach Barta glanced down at the back of his practice schedule.

"We're going to be on television for the championship, statewide," he continued. "Mr. Hobelmann and his guys are doing it, and it's really a big honor that they've been asked. We all know what a great job they do. What it means to us, guys, is that there are going to be pregame introductions and long TV time-outs.

"We're going to get knocked out of our routine. I want you to be prepared for that. I want you really, really to relax down there. You need to act like you're old bulls used to the bright lights. I got a feeling Olpe is going to be sky-high. Not us. We've been to this game before."

Coach Barta took a seat on his stool and gave his team a long searching look.

"This is a sentimental week," he told them. "It's the last time all of us are going to be together. It's the last time we get to sit in here together and talk. We'll do our last drills together."

He paused.

"I'm fired up, too, guys," he said. "You know I don't get that way often. I'm too old. But this is the week an old guy like me gets fired up."

He nodded to the freshmen on the east wall. One of them got up and turned off the lights. It was the last day of film for this edition of the Redmen, and Coach Barta was pulling no punches.

The first series of plays focused on the Eagles' offense, especially their passing game. The had a strong-armed quarterback named Matt Redeker, and his favorite target was a six-foot-three, two-hundred-pound tight end, Josh Klumpe, who was thought to be among the best receivers in the state.

"They're going after you, no. 1," said Coach Barta, calling out Ethan Eastes. "You might as well face it, E."

E did not move. He sat stone-faced as the Olpe passing plays raced before him.

"They know you've been beaten a couple of times," Coach Barta said. "You're small, and they're going to throw it at you."

When it was time to parse Olpe's defense, Coach Barta zeroed in on plays that were run to the Eagles' left side. He had recognized that the Eagles liked to line up their best athletes on the right side, and he knew that Olpe's coaching staff would be focused on shutting down Colt on that side. They had seen film, too, and were not going to let the kid who had already gained 1,650 yards beat them. Coach Barta was ready to run to their right side with Joe.

"We're going to run over that right end, aren't we, Kalen?" he asked Kalen Mace. "If you can't handle him, you're going to walk home from Hays. Your mother won't even love you."

The mood remained light all week at practice, and the Redmen hit just as hard as they had in the first week of training camp back in August. Coach Barta conceded that even some of his staff thought it was foolish to do so while preparing for a championship game. His team was battle tested after fifteen weeks of practice and twelve games. Why risk injury?

"I'm old, and I'm hardheaded," he told them.

One of the Redmen, in fact, did suffer a potentially critical injury: Joe Osburn had twisted his ankle. He did it, however, in the lunchroom on Wednesday afternoon, roughhousing with his teammates. He was barely able to jog.

Leo and the water boys kept the ice coming, but no one would know whether he could play until game day. Marshall, too, was taking it easy. He had not participated in the hitting drills since suffering his concussion in the opening game of the season. Against Meade, he got his bell rung again, making a tackle. It was not a concussion, but it had spooked him.

The All-Mid-Continent League teams had been selected earlier in the week, and after practice on the night before Thanksgiving Coach Barta told the Redmen how they had fared. "The coaches in the league treated us pretty good in the voting," he said. "But I want you guys to know that we think you're all All-Staters, and I wouldn't trade any one of you."

In fact, the Redmen dominated the All-League team. Colt and Joe were named first-team running backs, and Justin Nixon, Dillon Corbett, Logan Tuxhorn, and Kris Lehmann joined them on the line. On defense, Marshall, Colt, Dillon, Kris, and Trevor Rempe were first team.

"I feel bad for Travis," said Coach Barta of his quarterback, who received an honorable mention.

"I screw quarterbacks because I'm conservative until I need them. We're going to need you Saturday, Travis."

Coach Barta raised both hands above his head, making sure that his team was still with him.

"There's one more thing," he said. "I got a call from the Topeka newspaper, and they picked Justin to their Super 11 team, which means they think he's one of the best eleven players in the state."

The locker room erupted in applause and cheers. No one was louder than Big Hutch. Justin had been his project for the last four years. Big Hutch taught Justin technique, encouraged him when he wanted to quit, and told Justin at every opportunity that he was a big-time player. Justin was blushing, and the tiniest of smiles creased the corners of his mouth. Big Hutch snuck up behind him, and he put both hands on Justin's wide and beefy soldiers.

"I'm proud of you, Big Nix," he said, following the remark with a hug.

On Thanksgiving morning, the Redmen got a visit from R. D. Hubbard, the namesake of Hubbard Stadium. He was probably the richest man Smith Center had ever produced. He now divided his time between Ruidoso, New Mexico, where he owned Ruidoso Downs racetrack, and Palm Desert, California, where he owned Bighorn Golf Club. But R.D. still had family here and in Phillipsburg, and came home via his private jet most Thanksgivings for the family dinner. He had not missed a championship game, either, over the last four years. He commandeered the university suite in the press box that he built as part of the R. D. Hubbard press box at Fort Hays State. He was a Kansan through and through; Fort Hays, Butler, and Kansas State were all targets of his generosity.

R.D. was brief with the Redmen. He complimented them on what they had accomplished and talked about how proud he was of how they conducted themselves as young men. He wished them luck, too. No matter what, he reminded them, "You're our boys."

Before Coach Barta turned the Redmen loose to their families, he reminded them about what the day meant. "Thanksgiving is about being grateful for what you have," he said. "It's about family, and we're a family in here. I love each and every one of you, and I am grateful for you."

The snow started falling late on Thanksgiving night and continued into the morning. It stopped in time, however, for the Redmen's final practice of the season. In the stadium, the boys were in full pads and game uniforms. The last practice before a game was usually boring by design, meant only to hammer in assignments on special teams and provide an opportunity to go over any adjustments that had been made throughout the week. It was usually over in ninety minutes or so. But today no one was in a hurry to get off the field. This was the last practice ever for this edition of the Redmen.

The coaches were scattered around the field, talking to clusters of players. Nate Smith, Brock's brother-in-law, had the attention of Tim Wilson and some of the linemen. He had one more semester of student teaching here and then had to go find a real job. Now, Nate was pointing to the sideline by the 10-yard line.

"How many of you guys can say you gave your spleen for the Redmen?" he asked. "That's where I lost mine."

He actually had—in junior high—as he dove to tackle a running back and save a touchdown. Unfortunately, he had landed on the back of the runner's foot, hard enough to bleed internally. His spleen was yanked out in the following days.

Finally, about noon, Coach Barta herded his team inside. He went over the following morning's schedule. The bus was leaving from here at seven-thirty, and they would be at Lewis Field in Hays by nine o'clock. The Redmen would line up for introductions at ten minutes to twelve.

"We're going down there together, and do know, that everyone here is as important as everyone else," the coach said. "Be there for each other, guys. That's what life is all about. I want you to dream, and to dream big. When you dream big, great things happen."

———

The signs were spotted along Highway 36: STOCKTON 46–0, CLAFLIN 30–8, NORTON 51–13, ST. MARY'S 56–26, OAKLEY 56–0. They went on for six miles all the way to Athol; there were sixty-six of them, one for every game the Redmen had won during the streak. The signs gave Marshall goose bumps. No one was sleeping on the Redmen's bus; yesterday had been too long a day, and they were tired of waiting.

After practice Friday, they had killed part of the day at the Jiffy Burger and ate again as a team at the Pizza Hut. There, Mary VanderGeisen had bought them a cake in the shape of a football; KICK ASS was swirled in frosting. Earlier this morning, about a hundred folks had showed up at the four-way stop shortly after seven thirty to send the Redmen off to Hays. It was mainly parents and family, but Stacy Rempe had her cheerleaders out and a boom box playing music. When the Redmen's bus turned on Main Street, the cheerleaders unfurled a banner between the banks for the bus to break through.

It was the signs on Highway 36, however, that had really gotten the players' juices flowing as they made their way eighty-eight miles south to Lewis Field at Fort Hays State. Marshall tried to read his scouting report, but mostly he looked out the window. Colt listened to music. Justin, a perennial sleeper, sat upright and looked straight ahead. The usually quiet bus was humming with energy.

"When they reach all the way to Phillipsburg," said Mike Rogers of the victory scores, "then we will have accomplished something."

In what seemed like no time flat, the Redmen were stepping off the bus and onto Lewis Field. It was a bright sunny day, forty degrees, and the parking lot already was filling up with tailgaters. Marshall and the rest of the seniors had made this trip three previous times, but never as the main attraction. They could not help but smile as they walked from one goalpost to the other, wondering how much faster they could really run on this bright green cushion.

Lewis Field was cozy. It seated more than six thousand people and was circled by a low-slung limestone fence. It was the western part of the state's turn to be the home team, and so the Smith Center faithful—at least those who arrived early enough—got to sit on benches with seat backs. The Redmen were in the visitors' locker room, but it might as well have been the Bellagio in Las Vegas after all the cracker-box bathrooms and girls' gyms the team had endured over the course of the season.

During warm-ups, Lewis Field's sound system pumped up the nerves of both teams. Ozzy Osbourne, Metallica, and Busta Rhymes blared from the speakers. Colt seemed to cut a little harder on his pregame handoffs. Joe's head bopped involuntarily. He also felt no pain in his ankle. After the introductions, there were only a few minutes for the coaches to talk to the Redmen. Still, Coach Barta took his team to the locker room. He stayed on point.

"They're good-looking kids, and big strong athletes," he said of the Olpe Eagles. "We need to put them away early."

Big Hutch was even more succinct. "Can you hear me, guys?" he asked sotto voce.

They nodded.

"Kick their ass," he said, not much louder.

Brock knelt down on the floor among the players. He

bowed his head. "Everybody close your eyes, focus, and visualize what we're about to do," he told them.

The Redmen closed their eyes.

"We play this game today because you live in Smith Center, Kansas," he said, "in a community that loves you and watches over you. Each one of you was born to be Redmen."

He paused.

"Seniors, this is it," he said. "We play this game for you. This is the last time you will ever pull on a Redmen jersey. We thank you, and we will follow you to victory."

"We are?" he asked quietly.

"Redmen," they answered, just as soft, but reverent.

"We are?"

"Redmen." The response came back a little louder.

"WE ARE?" he roared.

"REDMEN" echoed everywhere.

The Smith Center faithful hardly had time to resettle in their seats after welcoming their boys onto the field before the Redmen struck. On the second play of the game, Joe Osburn slipped around Kalen Mace's block and went seventy-five yards for a touchdown, silencing Olpe's side of the field. Joe's ankle apparently was fine, and Coach Barta's game plan was sound.

The Eagles, however, were not easily intimidated. Their quarterback, Matt Redeker, led them right back downfield, hitting his big tight end, Josh Klumpe, twice. They were, indeed, going after Ethan Eastes. With the Redmen looking for a pass, Olpe's Cole Krueger bashed his way for five- and six-yard gains. Suddenly, the Eagles were on the Redmen's 19-yard line. On first down, Redeker dropped back, looking for Krueger in the flat, but this time, E had read the play beautifully and stepped in front of the pass for an interception. He was tackled immediately, but he popped up smiling with the ball aloft in his hand and Marshall, Colt, and Trevor piling on top of him.

Coach Barta had been correct about the right side of the Eagles' defense. It was stout and keyed on stopping Colt. The Redmen hammered at them on their next possession, but all it was doing was getting Colt beat up. The Redmen defense, meanwhile, was bending but not breaking. The Eagles were picking up first downs and growing emboldened by their passing game, so on fourth down and thirteen at the Redmen's 35-yard line, they went for it. Redeker connected with Krueger near the sideline, but Olpe was six inches short of the first down.

Joe Osburn needed just two plays to make them pay. He took the ball from Travis and zipped right through a wide hole blasted open by Cody and Van Tucker. Then he sailed into open field for a seventy-one-yard touchdown run.

When Olpe's Brad Argabright returned the ensuing kickoff eighty-three yards for a touchdown to bring the Eagles within a touchdown, it looked as if the Redmen might actually have a tussle.

Brooks Barta had come to the game with his wife, Tonya; his ten-year-old son, Mason; and his seven-year-old daughter, Tabor. But after the Olpe touchdown he left them in the grandstand and came to the sideline. He was in his own school colors, a blue "Holton" hat and windbreaker, but there was no doubt which team he was for. Brooks was no longer a high school coach but a Smith Center graduate and the son of a legend.

Before he let his offense return to the field, Coach Barta huddled them up and said, "Let's show them what Redmen football is all about."

They began the drive that Coach Barta had been setting up all year on their own 30-yard line. Trevor took a handoff up the middle; Colt another over left tackle; Trevor back up the middle; Joe right; and finally Trevor inside once more. Olpe—everyone in the state—had seen this rhythm before from the Redmen. It was bruising, power football. For thirty years, it had frustrated and exhausted teams. It powered the Redmen all the way down to Olpe's 25-yard line.

Facing third down and six, Coach Barta decided it was time to keep his promise to his quarterback. He whispered the play to Travis. On "Go," Travis faked a handoff to his brother, another one to Colt, and then skipped around right end. He went twenty-three yards before being pushed out of bounds at the Olpe 2-yard line.

Travis bounded back to the huddle as if he were on a trampoline. Still, the Eagles stiffened. They stopped Trevor once, twice, three times trying to power straight ahead. It was now fourth and goal, and Coach Barta called Travis's number again. This time, Travis turned left and faked to Trevor and Joe, then angled into the end zone untouched. It had taken twelve plays and more than five minutes, but the Redman were up, 20–7, with ten minutes left before the half.

The Eagles were deflated. They dragged back to their sideline. Now Coach Barta and the Redmen wanted to knock them out. After his defense held Olpe on another failed fourth-down conversion, Coach Barta called Travis back to the sideline. He put his arm on the quarterback's shoulder and leaned in with a play. There was a trace of a grin on Travis's face as he returned to the huddle. Simultaneously, Little Hutch walked down to John Terrill, Shane Mc-

Call, Dave Mace, and Jay Overmiller, all of whom were on the sidelines keeping stats.

"Here comes a touchdown," he said, holding his hand over the microphone of his headset.

When the ball was snapped it looked like any other Redmen running play, Travis handing the ball to Trevor and Olpe rushing to the middle of the Smith Center line. Except this time Trevor was empty-handed, and Travis had the ball cocked by his ear. He slung a pass downfield to Kris Lehmann, who was wide-open in the middle of the field. Kris pulled it in at Olpe's 25-yard line and ran into the end zone. It was only the eighteenth pass Travis had thrown all year, and it had gone fifty-seven yards for a touchdown.

Coach Barta had spent a whole season setting up that pass. The Eagles had started the game with eight and nine guys in the box, or near the line of scrimmage. Smith Center, they knew, rarely passed. By running the ball down the Eagles' throat on the previous drive, Coach Barta had ensured that every Olpe player would be as close to the line of scrimmage as possible.

Travis had started for the end zone as soon as he let go of the ball. He crashed into Kris in the end zone, and the Smith Center sideline was a jubilant mosh pit. When Marshall bolted through the line untouched for the two-point conversion, the Redmen had a 28–7 lead.

There were still nearly thirty-two minutes of football left to play, but at the moment no one doubted that Smith Center was going to win its sixty-seventh straight game to set the Kansas state record and capture its fifth straight title, to tie another record. When time finally did run out on the Redmen's 49–18 victory over Olpe, one of the most maligned senior classes in Kansas football history had left little doubt that they should forever be called one of the best.

Each senior had contributed mightily. Travis, who had been overlooked in All-League voting, had run for one touchdown and thrown for another. E had two interceptions and three solo tackles, and he had led a Redmen defense that had forced an Olpe fumble and stopped four fourth-down conversions. Trenton Terrill, not even all the way back from his knee injury, had pressured Redeker and notched a couple of tackles. Cody Tucker and Kalen Mace, largely unsung for most of the season, opened holes big enough for Joe Osburn to run 210 yards through.

When Joe's ankle finally gave out and he left the game, Marshall played tailback and ran for 138 yards and three more touchdowns. Two of Marshall's runs were the stuff of highlight reels as he leaped and twisted for fifty-four- and sixty-three-yard scores.

With about a minute left in the game, the chants from the grandstands of "Sixty-seven! Sixty-seven!" began. Coach Barta was standing next to Ethan Eastes and caught his eye.

"That was the best game you've ever played," the coach said. "How does it feel?"

Ethan smiled.

Justin looked for his folks in the stands with a beatific smile. Trevor and Travis had their arms around each other. Mike Rogers grabbed Colt and patted him. And Marshall had tears streaming down his face. The summers he had spent in the weight room, the hits he had taken, and all the times he had gotten chewed out were worth it.

"We did it," he said. "We did it."

When the captains led the seniors to the center of the

field to pick up the championship trophy, there were more tears from the folks wearing red. When Kris Lehmann hoisted it into the air and they all reached to touch it, there was a wonderful roar.

A half hour later, the Redmen returned to the locker room. They had earned the hugs and tears of their families and enjoyed the attention of the television and newspaper reporters.

The locker room had a long, narrow configuration that was not conducive to circling up. Still, the old men and little children of Smith Center kept pouring through the doors to be with their boys.

I searched up and down for the seniors. I wanted to remember their faces at this moment. Marshall. Justin. Kris. Trenton. Joe. Joel. Travis. Trevor. Kalen. Ethan. Cody. Brit. Colin. Johnny. Landon. They were not the most talented class in Redmen history, but they had worked hard and reached their potential, and together they were champions.

Then I saw my son, Jack, across the room. He reached across his chest in either direction and grasped the hands of the water boys as if he had been circling up all of his short life. Just as my heart leaped yet again, Coach Barta asked his son, Brooks, to address the team.

"I imagine you heard many times last fall, how to carry this experience in football to other aspects of life," Brooks said. "Relationships, academics, jobs, families. They require the same kind of commitment, sacrifice, preparation, toughness, and hard work.

"All of us will have opportunities to experience the same kind of success over and over. We have to make good choices about the people we surround ourselves with and commit to sharing our own experience and commitment to others."

I watched Jack watch Brooks. I watched Coach Barta listen to his son. I looked down the rows of fathers holding the hands of their boys. Coach Barta was more than just a helluva football coach.

# EPILOGUE

Life is not about winning or losing; it's about competing. It's about working hard and getting a little bit better each day.

—Roger Barta, December 1, 2008

Mary, Jack, and I were among the pilgrims who, upon their return from Hays, made the trek to Jones Machinery late on the night of the state championship to see the number "67" hoisted in the sky above Smith Center. Who knew that Christmas lights on a forklift in a gravel parking lot could light up the plains of Kansas and warm the hearts of its people? The Redmen's place in Kansas high school football lore was secure: Smith Center alone owned the state record for consecutive victories and now was one of only four teams that had won five consecutive state titles.

Those feats had prompted Ivan Burgess to send out a heartfelt message to the e-mail subscribers of the *Echo*, a rare "extra" edition.

"Well, we done it," Ivan began. "Sixty-seven wins in a row. New Kansas state record. Last year we graduated the 'dream' class. This year started out as a question mark. It ended with an exclamation point! Usually I'm pretty unemotional about football. I love to watch a good game. This year I wanted this team to win so bad that I almost got emotional about it. They had labored in the shadow of a great group of young men for several years. This was their year to move into the spotlight to either shine brilliantly or fade away.

"They chose to shine. This team wasn't the result of a September through November walk in the park. This team was the result of good old fashion work, work, work."

The following Monday, Coach Barta held a final meeting with his team as he had for the past thirty seasons. It was an opportunity for the seniors to impart some wisdom before they left their lockers on the west wall for good. Each took a turn telling the underclassmen how fast the four years had passed and how the fact that they were all sitting here in December with a championship trophy was evidence that hard work pays off. Quite a few of them had quivers in their voices when they thanked the coaches and their teammates.

Not Justin Nixon. His hair was combed, and he was clean-shaven. The next day he was heading to Topeka to get his photo taken with the ten other players whom the *Topeka Capital-Journal* had named the best in the state of Kansas. He had accomplished what he had set out to do at the beginning of the season and so much more.

"Enjoy it, guys," Justin said, a smile growing on his face, "because I'm already starting to miss it."

Coach Barta planted himself in the middle of the locker room and spoke to his Redmen as a team for the final time. "I'm getting up there in years, and there's not going to be too many of these left for me," he said. "I'm proud of our winning streak because it's the accumulation of a lot of great young men working their way around this room just as these seniors have.

"But I also want you to understand that life is not about winning or losing; it's about competing. It's about working hard and getting a little bit better each day."

Coach Barta pointed to the seniors on the west wall. He looked at them like he really was going to miss them. He had had several teams that were far more talented, but he was really proud of this bunch. "That is what these guys did," he said to the rest of his team. Then he walked a couple of steps toward the seniors, lifted his arms out to the side, and said, "I thank you for that."

Coach Barta next fixed his gaze on the juniors. He let his eyes meet each and every one of them. "I don't think the streak has to end if you guys follow their example," he told them.

By the following weekend, the Redmen's sixty-seven-game winning streak resonated far beyond the state of Kansas. There had been a celebration for the team scheduled on Sunday at Smith Center High School. In the previous forty-eight hours, however, the two teams in the nation ahead of Smith Center with the longest active high school football winning streaks had lost. On Friday, South Panola High School had its eighty-nine-game streak snapped in the Mississippi Class 5A state championship. The next day, Maryville High School was defeated in the Tennessee Class 4A title game, ending its string of victories at seventy-four games.

So now the Redmen were the high school team with the longest active victory streak in America. Hundreds of towns-people shuffled through the high school cafeteria to get foot-balls signed and to have photographs taken with team members. Marshall McCall, Kris Lehmann, Justin Nixon, Trenton Terrill, Travis and Trevor Rempe, and the rest of the seniors gathered for a team picture, knowing they had done all they could do for Redmen football—they were leaving here 53–0.

When college signing day arrived in February 2009, the talent and grit of this senior class received further notice. Marshall accepted a scholarship to play at Hutchinson Junior College, as did Kris Lehmann. Justin was not offered a scholarship to Kansas State, but Sterling College came up with enough scholarship and aid money to allow him to become the first Nixon to attend college. Justin will see many familiar faces; Trevor and Travis Rempe also accepted scholarships to play football there.

Only Joe Osburn was at loose ends as spring approached. In January, Joe made good on his promise to go to Kansas City to find his biological parents. He found them, but apparently they were not what he was looking for, so he returned to Smith Center after a couple of days. He had an offer from Sterling College, but he was thinking of joining the U.S. Marine Corps. Instead, in late spring, Joe accepted a football scholarship to Highland Community College. Joel, his adoptive brother, was going to Coffeyville Junior College on a football scholarship.

The Smith Center High School motto is WHERE TRADITION NEVER GRADUATES, and perhaps Coach Barta had this in mind one day in February when he showed up at Smith Center Elementary School with a state championship ring. That school's motto, fittingly, is WHERE THE TRADITION BEGINS. He took the ring to the classroom of Gavin Overmiller.

I heard about it in an e-mail from Jay Overmiller, who months before had told me how little boys in Smith Center grew up wanting to be Redmen, and how Redmen grew up to become champions. Jay had ordered the ring for Gavin.

"Talk about building character," Jay wrote. "Respect from the best. When I talked to Gavin that night he looked like he walked and talked ten foot tall. He now knows the feeling the rest of us know from playing for Coach Barta.

"It will be with him always."

# ACKNOWLEDGMENTS

Not long ago, I heard Doris Kearns Goodwin say that when she was writing her recent book about President Abraham Lincoln she woke up every day wanting to be a better person. I feel the same way because of my time with Roger Barta, his coaching staff, the players, their families, and the people of Smith Center, Kansas.

The community welcomed Mary, Jack, and me so warmly and completely that, even if I listed the Smith Center phone book in these acknowledgments, I'd be afraid I was leaving someone out. We left your town with so many friends and are so grateful for that. We thank you all for opening your homes and your hearts and giving us a once-in-a-lifetime experience.

I have listed the names of all the Redmen between these covers, and I wish I could have written at length about each and every one of you. It was my privilege and pleasure spending time with you. You are champions beyond the football field. Remember that you have friends in New York.

I do have to thank Betty Lambert, who was our landlady as well as friend and a fount of local history. Stacy Cole, "Miss Stacy," was the best first teacher Jack could ever have, and Marge Park and her play group were one of his favorite destinations. Ron Meitler is the superintendent for the school district and gave me the run of the schools, where I met many committed teachers. I thank you all for your kindness and inspiration.

Conor Nicholl is a young, talented reporter at the *Hays Daily News* who was an invaluable resource on Kansas high school football. John Baetz, a former Redman and the editor and publisher of *Kansas Pregame Magazine*, also pointed me in the right direction.

I could not have returned to high school without the indulgence and support of Tom Jolly, the sports editor of the *New York Times*. He has encouraged me to pursue many lines of reporting that have enriched my personal experiences and, I hope in some cases at least, our readers. I am proud to work alongside a talented bunch of editors and reporters in the sports department. I'm gratified that many of them also are true friends.

Alex Ward, the editorial director of book development at the *New York Times*, has been a wonderful supporter and constant source of wise advice. My editor at the Times Books imprint of Henry Holt and Company, Paul Golob, simply made this book better with his keen insights and deft editing touch. Thank you, Paul. His assistant, Kira Peikoff, kept me on track. I was lifted by the enthusiasm that Maggie Richards, Holt's director of sales and marketing, had for this project. I appreciate the hard work she and Nicole Dewey, director of publicity, continue to give to this book.

Robbie Anna Hare of Goldfarb & Associates has been my

friend and agent for a long time now. She brings good cheer and a sharp pencil to all of my projects. Robbie and Ron Goldfarb were especially enthusiastic about sending me back to Kansas. I'm glad they made it possible that I could. Thank you.

I am blessed to have good friends from Kansas City and Texas and other random places. You make me laugh and my life richer. I am bountifully blessed by a large, often unruly family of Drapes and Kennedys, which includes in-laws and out-laws, and nieces and nephews. You are big fun, and I love you all.

I want to remember Plott Brice and Jimmy Kennedy as well. Plott loved football as much as journalism and would have relished a Friday night in Hubbard Stadium. Jimmy was a sports enthusiast who worked at being a coach and believed competition was not about winning and losing but learning lessons for later. His boys, Christopher, Matthew, and Brian, are evidence that he imparted those concepts successfully.

Mary Kennedy and Jack Drape, I am grateful the most for you and how you have enriched every day of my life. I love you, and remember: WE ARE! REDMEN!

# ABOUT THE AUTHOR

Joe Drape is a reporter for the *New York Times* and the author of *The Race for the Triple Crown* and *Black Maestro*. A graduate of Southern Methodist University, he previously worked for the *Dallas Morning News* and the *Atlanta Journal-Constitution*. When he doesn't live in Kansas, he lives in New York City with his wife and son.